DEFEND
YOUR FAITH

100 DEVOTIONS
FOR KIDS WITH QUESTIONS

WRITTEN BY JESSE FLOREA

B&H
kids
Brentwood TN

Writer
Jesse Florea

Content Contributors
Tim Shoemaker
Dave Michael
Marianne Hering
Rachel Pfeiffer
Tim Wesemann
Tina Cho
Nathan Enger
Eva Marie Everson
Rhonda Robinson

Copyright © 2020 by B&H Publishing Group
All rights reserved.
Printed in China
May 2023

978-1-4627-9673-1

Published by B&H Publishing Group
Brentwood, Tennessee

Dewey Decimal Classification: J242.62
Subject Heading: DEVOTIONAL LITERATURE / APOLOGETICS / FAITH

Unless noted all Scripture quotations are taken from the Christian Standard Bible®,
copyright © 2017 by Holman Bible Publishers. Used by permission.
Christian Standard Bible® and CSB® are federally registered
trademarks of Holman Bible Publishers.

2 3 4 5 6 7 8 • 27 26 25 24 23

Contents

Introduction: Why Do You Believe in God?

Can you answer that question? Right now putting your beliefs into words may seem hard. But don't worry. The answer exists, and you can have confidence in your beliefs. When you put your faith in Jesus, you stand on the truth. Make that a capital T, because Jesus is the Truth (see John 14:6).

For thousands of years, followers of Christ have looked into the facts and built their faith on solid evidence. These brilliant thinkers studied history, science, philosophy, religion, theology, and culture. Then they put together a thoughtful apology. This was a *waaay* different apology than the one your parents tell you to give to your little sister after you hurt her feelings.

In this case *apology* comes from the Greek word *apologia*, which means "to give an answer" or "verbally defend." People who defend their beliefs in God with their words are called *apologists*.

One of Jesus' closest friends, Peter, used the word *apologia* when he wrote, "Do not fear what they fear or be intimidated, but in your hearts regard Christ the Lord as holy, ready at any time *to give a defense* to anyone who asks you for a reason for the hope that is in you" (1 Peter 3:14–15, emphasis added).

As a Christian, you have a hope that never fades. You have a foundation that never cracks. You have a Friend who never fails. But even with everything God gives you, you can sometimes feel unequipped to defend your faith. You might think you don't have all the answers or that you'll mess up the words. Those feelings are natural.

During your life, you'll grow as a defender of the faith. The more you talk about Jesus, the better you'll become at it. The more facts and truths you learn about Christianity, the easier it is to share those beliefs with others.

Don't be afraid to ask hard questions. Asking questions unlocks learning. Questions don't show your doubt; they express your desire to learn. It's important to ask questions about the world, the Bible, and your faith. It's even *more* important to know where to look for the answers.

The Bible is packed with answers about life's biggest questions and proof of the truth of God's Word. But you can also turn to trusted people in your life—parents, grandparents, pastors, and other family and church leaders—to find biblical wisdom. Reading devotional books like this one will help too!

Each of the entries in this book was designed to help you dig deeper into what it means to follow Christ and to help you answer the question, "Why do I believe in God?"

The simple answer is that it's the best and smartest way to live. God made you, loves you, forgives you, and gives purpose to your life. He protects and helps you while you're here on earth, and He also guarantees that you'll live forever with Him. Evidence for God is everywhere in creation, but you can also see Him in history and in the changed lives of people who follow Him.

The deeper truth is that everyone must answer the question of "Why do I believe in God?" for himself or herself.

As you learn more about *apologetics*, or defending your faith, you'll gain confidence in helping your friends and other people answer that question by looking at the facts. This devotional features lots of facts about God and the Bible under seven different headings. (These are the same categories you'll find in the bonus material of the *CSB Defend Your Faith Bible*.) Throughout the book, look for each of these icons:

KNOW QUESTIONS
Answering the Big Questions About God and the Bible
Here you'll find practical answers to some of the biggest questions about God, your life, and the Bible:

- *How do I know that the Bible is really true?*

- *What's the point of being a good person if bad stuff is going to happen anyway?*

SCIENCE IN THE BIBLE
Seeing God in His Creation
We can see God's design throughout science and Creation, and these devos will help you think through questions such as:

- *Can I study science in school and still believe in God?*

- *How does the orderliness of creation show there's a God?*

GOOD WORDS
Bible Vocabulary
Understanding more Bible vocabulary can help you speak up for what you believe and answer some of your friend's questions about what makes Christianity unique, such as:

- *What does* idol *mean in my world today?*

- *Are angels what I think they are?*

DIGGING INTO THE WORD

Evidence to Trust in the Bible

The people, places, and events described in the Bible are real. This section will help you answer questions about the historical accuracy of God's Word, such as:

- *Do archaeological finds prove that the people in the Bible were real?*

- *How do artifacts show us what life was like for early Christians?*

DEFENDERS OF THE FAITH

Real People, Real Faith

From Bible times to modern days, many Defenders of the Faith have stood up for God's truth. Read about them and then hear about a few Defamers of the Faith who failed to follow-through in making good decisions. You'll learn:

- *How can my faith make a difference in the world if I'm just a kid?*

- *What other real Christians have overcome hard times?*

UNTWISTING SCRIPTURE

Finding the Consistent Truth of God's Word

God's Word never contradicts itself, and He wants you to know the truth. These devotions offer answers to questions such as:

- *Don't some Bible verses have opposite messages?*

- *How do I understand the hard parts I read in the Bible?*

THAT'S A FACT

Fun Facts with a Deeper Meaning

These devotions are filled with surprising facts and statistics from God's Word and His world. After reading these devos, you'll better answer questions like:

- *What did Jesus say on the cross?*

- *Why is life filled with so many tests?*

As you read through this book (and even when you're done!), write down the questions you have about God and the Bible. You can use the note pages at the end of this book.

Remember, having questions is a good thing! God is so big, so powerful, and so awesome that you will never know everything about Him. But asking questions and looking for answers will keep you on the firm path of following Him.

Never stop searching for answers. Every time you read through the Bible, you'll learn a little more. Older Christians and your parents can also help lead you to the truth. You can even pick up a Bible dictionary or concordance to look up Scriptures or other information on topics from God's Word. The truth is out there, and you'll find it in your relationship with Jesus Christ.

And as you grow and learn, you'll become even better equipped to know how to defend your faith!

Eva couldn't believe how much the Bible came to life as she toured Israel. At this very moment, she stood in Tel Hazor National Park in the northeastern part of the country.

"This is where Joshua fought King Jabin," a park director said through an interpreter. "This is where you can see Jabin's palace."

For more than seventy years, archaeological teams have uncovered artifacts throughout Tel Hazor. They've found storehouses for food, stables for horses, and pieces of King Jabin's armor. But one of the most significant findings occurred in 2012 when they uncovered the sooty remains of burned wheat and buildings that matched the Bible's description of a famous battle (Joshua 11:1, 10–11).

The book of Joshua explains how Joshua led God's people (the Israelites) into the Promised Land. King Jabin, who lived in the north, called together all the other kings in the region to fight against Joshua. Jabin thought he could build an army stronger than the Israelites. He was wrong. God was on the side of His people, so the battle was over before it began. Joshua 11 describes how the Israelites captured Hazor, killed Jabin, and burned the city.

Eva and her friends followed their guide into a deep, rocky ditch to see a piece of Bible history from 3,400 years ago. At the bottom, the guide pointed to a deposit of soot sandwiched among layers of rocks.

"Touch the burned palace of Jabin," the interpreter said.

Eva couldn't believe his offer. She put one hand on a boulder and stretched over a roped-off area.

Suddenly, the park director stood by her side. "You are touching the Bible," he said in perfect English.

Surprised, Eva's hand slipped, and her feet flew into the air. She ended up not just touching the Bible; Eva literally fell into God's Word!

Some take pride in chariots, and others in horses, but we take pride in the name of the LORD our God.—Psalm 20:7

DEFEND YOUR FAITH

God wants *you* to fall into the Bible too. You don't have to travel to Israel and slip on a rock. But as you read the Bible, look up the cities on a map. See how God led His people through the Promised Land or follow how Paul traveled to spread God's truth in Acts.

When you dig into God's Word, you'll discover these were *real* men and women. *Real* kings and queens. You can trust the stories, just like you can trust God. Many people, like King Jabin, put their faith in possessions and power. Be different. Be wise. Take pride in discovering more about your faith and the one true God.

BIBLES BY BALLOON

Annie lives in South Korea. Although her country has some of the largest churches in the world, she often thinks about her neighbors to the north. North Korea is a Communist country. The government controls all the TV shows, Internet, and churches. People who live there aren't allowed to worship God.

Christianity in North Korea is basically outlawed. Families who do follow Christ are often fired from jobs, thrown in jail, tortured, or starved. Many people in North Korea feel hopeless. Annie wants to give them hope.

Since she was nine years old, Annie, her dad, and friends from church have sent God's Word into North Korea in an interesting way—by balloon!

Annie and other volunteers cover small Bibles in bubble wrap. Then they put stickers on the packages to explain what's inside. Annie also unwraps hundreds of digital memory cards and helps upload a Bible for North Koreans onto each card. The Bibles and memory cards get attached to gigantic balloons.

Volunteers wait for the perfect night and weather conditions to fill the balloons with air and send them into North Korea. Some of the balloons fly higher than airplanes! A GPS system tracks the balloons as they drift into North Korea. Sometimes Annie imagines a person coming across one of the balloons in a field or dusty dirt road. She knows that God's Word changes lives and that God is in control of whatever happens when the balloons land.

"My word that comes from my mouth will not return to me empty, but it will accomplish what I please and will prosper in what I send it to do."—Isaiah 55:11

DEFEND YOUR FAITH

The Bible changes lives. Annie knows some North Koreans who have found the balloon-delivered Bibles, believed in Jesus, and accepted God's truth. Some of them have escaped into South Korea to start a new life because of the hope they found in one of the Bibles she helped send.

How do you share God's Word with the people in your life? When you tell others the truth that's found in the Bible, it always accomplishes God's purposes. If a friend is feeling down, you can give her words of hope. If a cousin likes to cuss, you can encourage him to watch his words by quoting a Bible verse.

Look for different ways you can share your faith and the power of the Bible with people you know. And be creative! Because who knew that a balloon could bring others into a relationship with Jesus?

DEFENDER FACTS
NAME: *ANNIE*
PLACE: *SOUTH KOREA*
TIME: *MODERN-DAY*

THE TRUTH ABOUT BEING FALSE

Do you like taking tests with true-or-false questions? Researchers have found the answer is more often *true* than *false*. But these tests can be tricky. The next time you have to answer a true-or-false question, remember these tips.

Tip 1: Read the questions carefully. If you skim, you may miss an important detail that makes the answer obvious.

Example: God told Moses to build an ark made of gopher wood. True or False?

The answer is false because Noah built the ark—not Moses. If you read too quickly, you could miss that detail.

Tip 2: If one part of the question is false, the answer is false.

Example: After Jesus rose from the dead, His disciples were all killed for their belief that He was God's Son. True or False?

The answer is false. Although many of them were killed for their beliefs, the Bible isn't clear how some others died, including John, who was imprisoned on the isle of Patmos.

Tip 3: Watch out for qualifying words, such as *always*, *all*, *only*, and *never*.

Example: Only Moses saw God in the Old Testament. True or False?

The answer is false because Jacob said he saw God (Genesis 32:30). The prophet Isaiah also recorded seeing God in Isaiah 6:1.

These test-taking tips can help you get an A in school. But it's even more important to test what you hear about God.

There will be false teachers among you. They will bring in destructive heresies, even denying the Master who bought them, and will bring swift destruction on themselves.—2 Peter 2:1

Defend Your Faith

The Bible warns us to beware of **false** teachers. These people twist truth and mislead people. For thousands of years, false teachers have made up rules or added to God's Word to lead people the wrong way. Some teachers have done this to get rich or powerful.

Whenever you hear someone teaching about God—whether it's a pastor, family member, or friend—test what they say versus what you know from God's Word. The key here is you must *know God's Word*. That's why reading the Bible yourself is so important. If you don't know the full truth, you can get misled by false teaching. So test everything you hear about God. When you find His truth, you'll get an A in life.

How would you like to have a built-in squirt gun on your body? Or maybe you'd like to walk around with an upside-down backpack stuck to your stomach for special storage?

If those ideas sound strange, you can thank God for His wisdom at creation. When God created the universe with His words, He had a perfect plan. He didn't make humans with our mouths facing up and a third arm sticking out of our chests. He designed everything with purpose. You can see the order of creation and the wisdom behind His design everywhere . . . especially in animals.

Take the archerfish. By the sound of its name, you might think it's an aquatic Robin Hood that shoots arrows to hunt food. But instead of arrows, God gave this tiny fish the ability to shoot water six feet into the air! This finned fellow also has amazing eyesight that allows it to hit its mark, even as the fish sits just below the water. When the archerfish spots a spider or an insect sitting on a branch near a lake, it shoots a jet of water from its mouth. The water zooms through the air and knocks the bug into the water. Then the archerfish gulps down its meal.

The wombat is an Australian oddity. Picture a tiny, hairy pig-bear with long claws. Wombats are marsupials, like kangaroos, so their babies are born tiny and grow in their mother's pouch. But instead of an upward-facing pouch, like other marsupials, God made a wombat's pouch open upside-down. Because wombats are great diggers who spend much of their lives underground, a normal pouch would quickly fill with dirt when the mother was digging. But a rear-facing pouch keeps the babies safe and clean.

God created the large sea-creatures and
every living creature that moves and swarms
in the water, according to their kinds. He also
created every winged creature according to
its kind. And God saw that it was good.
—Genesis 1:21

DEFEND YOUR FAITH

Scientists who believe in evolution claim all living creatures slowly evolved and developed unique characteristics over time. But how would an archerfish eat without its squirt gun? And how could wombat babies survive if their mothers had normal pouches? If God hadn't given these amazing animals their unique skills and designs from the time He created them, they never would have survived. The truth is, God had a plan. He knew exactly what He was doing, even if it looked a little weird.

And remember this: The same God who came up with these awesome designs made you too. You're made perfect . . . even if you don't have a built-in squirt gun.

DOES GOD GET TIRED?

How much do you sleep every night? When you were much smaller, you slept about sixteen hours a day. That's a lot! You probably sleep less now that you're older, and you probably drool less too.

Koalas aren't known for their drool. But they are excellent sleepers. These tree-dwelling, bear-looking, eucalyptus-eating Australian animals can sleep twenty-two hours a day. Brown bats sleep nearly twenty hours, and adult tigers doze for sixteen hours a day.

Because God created us in His image, some people wonder if God ever gets tired or sleeps. After all, the Bible says God "rested on the seventh day from all his work that he had done" (Genesis 2:2). Creating a bridge of interlocking plastic bricks on the kitchen table is hard enough, so creating the entire universe must have been super tiring!

Not for God. God is spirit. He is not confined to a physical body. He existed before time began. He actually made *time* (try to wrap your head around that). Even though He created humans and animals to sleep and tells us to rest, God doesn't sleep. Nothing happens without Him knowing about it. He's always alert and always ready to hear our prayers.

If someone asks you if God gets tired, you can confidently say, "No way! He's all-powerful and looking out for us all the time."

When the Bible says God *rested*, it simply means He stopped what He was doing. God has a purpose for everything He does. When He stopped on the seventh day of creation, He wasn't tired. He was finished. And then He rested to be an example to us of the importance of rest in our lives.

The LORD is the everlasting God, the Creator of the whole earth. He never becomes faint or weary; there is no limit to his understanding.
—Isaiah 40:28

DEFEND YOUR FAITH

God never gets tired. He never needs rest. That's important to know, because it means He's always available to help us and always aware of what's happening to us.

When you pray to God, no matter where you live, He hears what you say. If you wake up in the middle of the night, you can talk to Him. If you're worried about a test in the middle of the afternoon, He's there to calm your fears. He's always watching over you, twenty-four hours a day, 365 days a year. His power never decreases. His energy never diminishes. His love never declines.

You might not be able to sleep as well as a koala, but you can sleep well for a human, knowing that God is always there.

A True Winner

The Bible is full of sports talk.

Don't believe it? Then why does God start off His book with a baseball reference: "In the *big inning* God created . . ." Sorry—that joke was a swing and a miss. Speaking of swinging, David served up some wise words about tennis in Psalm 84:10: "Better a day in your courts than a thousand anywhere else." Joseph also served in Pharaoh's court (Genesis 41:46), so tennis seems to be a Bible favorite.

Track probably shows up more than any other sport. Beginning in Genesis, we learn that Adam was the fastest runner because he was first in the human race. Ha!

Enough of the jokes. Because, seriously, the apostle Paul often referred to running races in the New Testament. He compared the runners and the races to living a life following Jesus.

Some of his metaphors are easy to follow, like when he writes, "Forgetting what is behind and reaching forward to what is ahead, I pursue as my goal the prize promised by God's heavenly call in Christ Jesus" (Philippians 3:13–14). Verses like those encourage us to pursue one goal: to follow God's call on our lives. Our past actions and mistakes don't matter. We need to live and make future decisions that bring glory to God. As we run the race to reach the goal of heaven, we can't do it on our own. We need Jesus and His victory!

But some of Paul's words can confuse people and easily be taken out of context. A good example is 1 Corinthians 9:24: "Don't you know that the runners in a stadium all race, but only one receives the prize? Run in such a way to win the prize." When some people read that verse, they think it means they'll be a failure if they don't win.

That's not the way God sees it. And that's not the way Paul saw it either. When he tells us to run to win the prize, he's telling us to give our best and not give up.

Don't you know that the runners in a stadium
all race, but only one receives the prize? Run
in such a way to win the prize.
—1 Corinthians 9:24

DEFEND YOUR FAITH

"Second place is just the first loser." Have you heard that quote before or seen it on a T-shirt? An athlete said those words after winning a race. A lot of times it seems like sports is all about winning.

The Bible may use sports metaphors, but living for God isn't a competition that can be won or lost. We're all winners when we give our hearts to God. He loves us the same, whether we're lifting the Super Bowl trophy or cleaning the toilet bowl for our family.

So fight through your struggles, confidently tell others about your faith, and make it your goal to finish strong for Him.

How many state capitals can you think of? Write down as many as you can in two minutes. If you can correctly name ten, that's more than most people can guess.

Some capital cities have special meanings behind their names. Sacramento, the capital of California, was named after the Sacramento River. A Spanish explorer gave the river its name in 1808. *Sacramento* is translated "Holy Sacrament," which is another name for taking communion to remember Jesus' Last Supper and sacrifice on the cross.

The names of biblical cities have special meanings too. Can you think of the three cities that played a major part in Jesus' life?

They are Bethlehem, Nazareth, and Jerusalem.

• *Bethlehem* means "house of bread." The city is mentioned in the first book of the Bible as the burial place of Rachel (Genesis 35:19). Later in the Old Testament, the prophet Micah said the Messiah would be born in Bethlehem (Micah 5:2). Jesus couldn't control where He was born. But God planned for His Son to be born in Bethlehem, so it's not surprising that this "house of bread" is where the "bread of life" (John 6:35) came to earth.

• *Nazareth* means "branch." It was such a small, unimportant town that it isn't even mentioned in the Old Testament. But several Old Testament prophets referred to the coming Messiah as "branch." Isaiah 11:1 says a "branch" will come from the family line of Jesse and bear fruit. Jesse was King David's father, and Jesus *was* from that family. Zechariah said God's servant would be called "branch" (Zechariah 3:8 and 6:12). Jeremiah 33:15 also referenced a "Righteous Branch" that would sprout up for David. Jesus lived in "branch" for nearly His entire childhood. Later in life, Jesus called Himself the vine that His followers branch off of (John 15:1–6).

• *Jerusalem* means "city of peace." This city is where Jesus was crucified on a cross and rose from the dead three days later. The Bible tells us Jesus *is* our peace (Ephesians 2:14). Jesus brought us peace with God by dying for our sins and rising from the dead (Romans 5:1) in the city of peace!

Since we have been justified by faith, we have peace with God through our Lord Jesus Christ.—Romans 5:1

DEFEND YOUR FAITH

When we "eat" the bread of life, we're never spiritually hungry again. As we branch off from the true vine, we thrive and produce spiritual fruit. And when we believe by faith in the Prince of Peace, we have peace with God. All three of these facts are reflected in the cities where Jesus lived.

These hidden treasures—and many others—were masterminded by God to help us understand more about Him. As you read your Bible, try to find out the meaning of the names of people and places you read about. Then see what great things God wants to show you through their names!

DID JESUS EVER GET IN TROUBLE WITH HIS PARENTS?

Jesus was the perfect child. Really, He was perfect. He never sinned, never went against God's rules, and always honored what His earthly parents said. But that doesn't mean He never got in trouble.

The Bible doesn't provide many details about what Jesus was like as a boy . . . until a situation came up when He was twelve years old. You can read about it in Luke 2:41–52.

Every year Mary and Joseph traveled with lots of other people from Nazareth to Jerusalem for the Passover Festival. Large crowds journeyed together. The adults helped each other watch the children, even if they weren't their own. On the way home after the festival, Jesus' parents didn't see Him for a while. At first Mary and Joseph weren't concerned, because they figured Jesus was with other families having fun as they walked. But after a day, they got worried. They headed back to Jerusalem. After three days had passed, they found Jesus in the temple listening to the religious leaders and asking them questions. Everyone was amazed at what this twelve-year-old knew and the answers He gave.

Jesus' parents were naturally panicky. "Son, why have you treated us like this?" Mary asked.

Jesus politely responded, "Why were you searching for me? Didn't you know that it was necessary for me to be in my Father's house?"

Mary and Joseph didn't understand what He meant, but they probably gave Him a joyful hug anyway. Then Jesus returned home with them and continued to obey and love them.

"Whoever does the will of God is my brother and sister and mother."—Mark 3:35

DEFEND YOUR FAITH

Have you ever wondered what it'd be like to have Jesus as a brother? Would He always be correcting you? It would be cool that He'd treat you kindly and never play with your toys without asking.

Of course, it would also be sad. The reason Jesus came to earth was to die on the cross for our sins and rise from the dead so we could be forgiven.

Actually, we sort of already know what it'd be like to have Jesus as a brother. Jesus said, "Whoever does the will of God is my brother and sister" (Mark 3:35). When you believe in Jesus as your Savior, you're part of God's family!

Although Jesus never disobeyed His parents, He knows we'll mess up all the time. But instead of getting in trouble with God, we will always find forgiveness when we confess our sins to Him. With God's Son as our brother and God as our heavenly Father, we're accepted . . . and they're always ready with a joyful hug.

WATER, WATER, EVERYWHERE

The story of Noah's ark is one of the most well known in the Bible. In the book of Genesis, it explains how it rained cats and dogs—well, two cats and two dogs. Then the giant ark shifted from *park* to *float*, and everything on earth was covered with water.

The Bible is clear that the flood covered the entire planet, but some people don't accept God's Word at its word. They argue the flood was a more regional event.

So what's the truth? A lot of science points to the biblical account of a global flood. A flood of biblical proportions would've kicked up a massive amount of rock sediment as vast watery depths poured out and the floodgates of the sky were opened (Genesis 7:11). That means water spewed out of springs in the earth and also fell from clouds. For forty days the water increased until the ark rose above the earth. All the waves and water would have moved around this rock sediment, until things calmed down and the sediment settled on the ocean's floor. And that's what modern-day scientists have found.

Geologists love to study the Grand Canyon in Arizona, because the different layers of rock can easily be seen. They discovered a specific type of rock called Tapeats Sandstone at the base of the Grand Canyon. This same layer of rock can be found in Wisconsin and more than six thousand miles away in Israel and Libya. A smaller, oops-I-left-the-water-running-in-the-bathtub type of flood never could've deposited the same layer of rock across such a vast area in multiple countries. These scientists believe the best explanation for this layer of rock is a worldwide flood as described in the Bible.

Then the water surged even higher on the earth, and all the high mountains under the whole sky were covered.—Genesis 7:19

DEFEND YOUR FAITH

Picture books sometimes make Noah's ark seem like a floating zoo. A smiling giraffe sticks its head out of the top of the boat as monkeys swing on the sides.

But the ark was anything but a pleasure cruise. It was God's judgment for sin. Before the flood, the Bible says "every inclination of the human mind was nothing but evil all the time" (Genesis 6:5). Things were so bad that God told Noah every creature on earth would be destroyed in the flood, except for Noah, Mrs. Noah, their three boys, their boys' wives, and the animals God brought into the ark.

Sin is serious. It separates us from God. Sometimes people get so caught up in their sin that they completely ignore God and act wickedly.

Fortunately for us, Noah's story doesn't end in destruction. It ends with a colorful rainbow and God's promise not to destroy the world by flood again. God gave the world a fresh start, and He did the same for us when He sent Jesus to earth to be our Savior.

# ARE DINOSAURS MENTIONED IN THE BIBLE?

The Bible includes many stories about *small armies*, but has no references to a T-Rex with *small arms*. Sometimes people in the Bible were described as stiff-necked, but there's no mention of a long-necked Brachiosaurus. The word *dinosaur* doesn't even appear in the Bible because it wasn't made up until 1842. Dinosaur comes from the Greek language and means *terrible lizard*.

Today, dinosaur bones fill museums. Paleontologists dig up dinosaur fossils all over earth and try to piece together what these massive creatures would've looked like. Books are filled with illustrations of dinosaurs and theories of how they behaved. Popular animated cartoons and movies feature dinosaurs running around and even talking (although there's definitely *no* scientific evidence that these creatures spoke).

Many kids have a fascination with dinosaurs. So what does the Bible say?

God created *all* the land animals, which would have included dinosaurs, on the sixth day of creation (Genesis 1:24–25). The Bible also mentions some dragon-like, dinosaur-ish beasts. Most of these are water creatures—not land animals. The *leviathan* described in Job 41; Job 3:8; Psalm 74:13–14; Psalm 104:26; and Isaiah 27:1 is a large, fierce sea creature. Job 40:15–24 gives details of the mighty *behemoth*. This creature ate grass, had a tail like a cedar tree, and was the "foremost of God's works." Then Isaiah 30:6 speaks of a flying fiery serpent.

Are any of these animals a dinosaur? Maybe. The Bible doesn't give a definitive description. But we do know that if dinosaurs roamed the earth, God was the One who created them.

DEFEND YOUR FAITH

God is bigger, greater, and more powerful than our human brains will ever understand. Of course, that doesn't stop humans from *trying* to know more about God. Seeking after God's truth is a good thing. That's what you're doing now by reading this book.

But in the book of Job, when he and his friends were trying to figure out why all sorts of bad stuff was happening to him, God asked Job, "Where were you when I established the earth? Tell me, if you have understanding" (Job 38:4). Did Job *have understanding*? No. Neither Job nor anyone else in the history of the world can answer that question with a *yes*.

There are some things we just won't know while we're here on earth. Scientists have theories about dinosaurs, but nobody knows for sure what they may have looked like or how they behaved. Dinosaurs are fun to think about. Just make sure your beliefs in these terrible lizards align with the Word of God.

A PICTURE OF ENDURANCE

Over just two years, Ernest Shackleton and twenty-nine men faced shipwrecks, hundred-foot waves, and numerous other near-death experiences. The sailors, explorers, and scientists who boarded a ship called *Endurance* in August 1914 knew their journey would be hard. Their goal was to be the first team to cross Antarctica—a 1,500-mile trek. But when they left England, the crew had no idea how appropriately their ship was named.

Less than six months into their journey, a giant ice floe just below the Antarctic Circle trapped their ship. The men hoped the ice would eventually break up. It didn't. Eleven months passed. Finally, ice crushed the *Endurance*. Shackleton and his men saved two lifeboats rigged with sails and dragged them for miles to the edge of the floe. In April 1916, the men piled into the lifeboats and spent twelve days at sea—constantly wet, freezing, and bailing water. Miraculously, they reached uninhabited Elephant Island and built a shelter. They were on land, but they knew nobody would find them there. Their only chance of rescue was to sail seven hundred impossibly dangerous miles to a whaling station on South Georgia Island.

Shackleton took one lifeboat and five men. They battled hurricane-force winds, hundred-foot waves, and bitter cold. Seventeen days later they made it to South Georgia Island. That was the good news. The bad news? The whaling station was on the far side of the island, and the lifeboat was too damaged to make it. Shackleton didn't give up. He climbed an uncharted mountain range and arrived at the whaling station, where he organized a rescue ship. In the end, every one of his men survived.

Consider it a great joy, my brothers and sisters, whenever you experience various trials, because you know that the testing of your faith produces endurance. And let endurance have its full effect, so that you may be mature and complete, lacking nothing.
—James 1:2–4

DEFEND YOUR FAITH

Life can be hard. You probably won't have to battle the freezing cold like Ernest Shackleton, but the Bible says you will experience trials. You may feel like an outcast because of your faith. You could have a family member get cancer. Accidents, epidemics, and natural disasters can throw unexpected obstacles in your life and cause you to doubt God.

When our faith is tested, that's when we must develop *endurance*—the ability to keep going when things are tough. Instead of giving up on God during hard times, we need to follow Him even more. We must trust the promises in His Word and keep looking at Jesus—the ultimate example of endurance, because of what He endured on the cross for us.

Endurance helps make us mature. So stay committed to Christ in the face of difficulty. Be strong. Don't quit. And most of all . . . remember Jesus rescues all who follow Him.

"Buts" of the Bible, Part 1

In many Bibles the word *but* appears nearly four thousand times. It's such a small word that it's easy to ignore. But one little *but* can make a big impact on a story and in your life.

When God rescued the Israelites from a life of slavery in Egypt, He had great plans for them. He promised to give them their own land so they'd have homes, animals, and plenty of good food. Some very wicked people already lived in the land, but God promised to help the Israelites successfully eliminate them.

With Moses leading the Israelites, they walked across a desert and to the edge of the Promised Land. Moses sent twelve scouts to explore the territory. When the scouts came back, all the Israelites gathered around to hear the report. The scouts told wonderful stories of a bountiful land. Ten of them also warned of strong, walled cities and the giants who lived there. Two of the scouts, Joshua and Caleb, encouraged the people to trust God. Caleb even reminded the Israelites that God would give them the land.

What happened next changed the future of a generation of people. The Bible says, "But the men who had gone up with him responded, 'We can't attack the people because they are stronger than we are!'" (Numbers 13:31).

Did you notice the word *but* in that verse? God had promised to drive out the wicked and give His people the land. God had demonstrated He had the power to do it by freeing the Israelites from Egypt, parting the Red Sea, and performing other miracles.

But the people forgot that and listened to the ten scouts. They complained against God, wishing they'd died in the desert rather than having to face the giants.

God gave them their wish. That generation of adults never saw the Promised Land. God had them wander the desert for forty years until their children were old enough—and wise enough—to trust God and conquer the Promised Land.

"Above all, be strong and very courageous to observe carefully the whole instruction my servant Moses commanded you. Do not turn from it to the right or the left, so that you will have success wherever you go."—Joshua 1:7

DEFEND YOUR FAITH

Sometimes God wants to take us places we've never been before. Places that will be good for us. But instead of trusting Him and moving forward, we think of reasons to be fearful. Sometimes when the word *but* is in the Bible, it's about people making excuses not to follow God. Joshua followed God, trusted in His promises, and had great success. Let's be careful not to let our excuses—our *buts*—stop us from enjoying God's plans for us!

"BUTS" OF THE BIBLE, PART 2

Many of the nearly four thousand *buts* in the Bible simply transition from one part of a story to another. But some *buts* are special because they're followed by an especially powerful word: *God*. A quick search through God's Word shows that "but God" appears more than forty times. When you see those words together, pay attention because God is at work.

God certainly did a lot of work in David's life. As a shepherd boy, David was picked by the prophet Samuel to be the next king of Israel. Soon after, the current king, Saul, invited David to play the harp in the palace. David earned the king's favor and became best friends with the king's son, Jonathan. David always trusted God, even believing that God would help him kill a nine-foot giant. (God did!) After killing Goliath, David became famous all over Israel. He won many other battles too. That made Saul extremely jealous. He tried to kill David more than ten times and even threw a spear at him—twice!

David was forced to run for his life. The Bible says, "Saul searched for him every day, but God did not hand David over to him" (1 Samuel 23:14).

Did you notice the *but* in that verse? Saul was the most powerful man in Israel. He had thousands of soldiers at his command. *But* he couldn't find David because God wouldn't let him. The same God who gave David victory over a giant kept David safe from an angry king. You can read 1 Samuel 16–31 for David's twisty and turny journey to the throne.

Yours, LORD, is the greatness and the power and the glory and the splendor and the majesty, for everything in the heavens and on earth belongs to you.—1 Chronicles 29:11

DEFEND YOUR FAITH

David faced a lot of troubles in his life. There will be times when we might feel surrounded by trouble too. We may not have to kill a giant and avoid spears, but we all face hard times. Bad things.

At times David felt God had abandoned him. He poured out his feelings in many psalms. But in his heart, David knew God was always with him, always protecting and guiding him. Near the end of David's life, he called the people together. He'd been a faithful king, and now it was time for his son, Solomon, to take the crown. David prayed a powerful prayer that starts in 1 Chronicles 29:11. Looking back at his life, David saw the struggles, but he also saw the Lord was in control the whole time. When you face difficulties, remember these words: *But God.* We have a rescuer—a Savior. We need to focus on Him, not the seeming impossibility of the situation. And like David, we need to look back at the major events in our lives. God was there with us! Can you imagine what might have happened to you . . . *but God?*

DOES IT DO ANY GOOD TO DO GOOD?

Sometimes when we do good things, nobody notices. Maybe you cleaned your room or helped a brother or sister with homework. Maybe you went out of your way to say something nice to the kid nobody talks to at school. If you don't get a "thank you," you might wonder, *What good is it to do good?*

People have been feeling that way for thousands of years. In the book of Esther, we read about Mordecai. He did a *really* good thing, but nobody seemed to notice.

Mordecai grew up in Jerusalem, until the Babylonians defeated the nation of Judah and took him prisoner. He was forced to live in a foreign country ruled by King Xerxes. One day, outside the king's gate, Mordecai overheard two guards planning to murder the king. Mordecai got word to King Xerxes, and the ruler was saved.

Mordecai did a good thing. You'd think the king's advisors would have rewarded him. Maybe they'd name a street after Mordecai or build a statue in his honor, right? But all they did was record his act in the royal diary (Esther 2:23). The good deed Mordecai did was all but forgotten. So what good did it do to do good?

Plenty, because God didn't forget.

Time passed. Things weren't going well for Mordecai. One of the king's top men, Haman, got very angry with Mordecai. Why? Because Mordecai didn't kneel down when Haman walked past. Jews, like Mordecai, knew they should kneel only before God. Haman made a wicked plan to hang Mordecai—and kill every other Jew in the country. That same night the king couldn't sleep. He had someone read the royal diary to him. When he heard how Mordecai had saved his life but never been rewarded, the king got busy. The next day the king had a parade for Mordecai and made Mordecai his special advisor.

At just the right time, Mordecai was saved, Haman was defeated, and the Jews were rescued.

*The eyes of the LORD roam throughout
the earth to show himself strong for those
who are wholeheartedly devoted to him.*
—2 Chronicles 16:9

DEFEND YOUR FAITH

Mordecai's story reminds us that God notices when we do good things—*even when nobody else does*. We don't do good things for the accolades or to win Student of the Month. We do good things for the simple reason that they're the right things to do. When we're wholeheartedly devoted to Christ, we're called to be kind even to those who aren't kind to us.

The apostle Paul put it best in 1 Corinthians 10:24: "No one is to seek his own good, but the good of the other person." So don't do good and wait for a "thank you." Let God be the One to reward you in His time. And remember . . . God doesn't forget.

FEARFUL AND FAITHFUL FOLLOWER

Gideon trusted God enough to go into battle with only three hundred men against an army of more than 120,000. It's one of the most amazing stories in the Old Testament (see Judges 7). That obedience earned him a shout-out in Hebrews 11, which is sometimes called the "Bible Hero Hall of Fame."

When we think of heroes, we usually picture someone who's fearless, strong, and powerful. But one of the biggest reasons we consider Gideon a hero was because he did the right thing . . . when he was scared.

In fact, that's the first thing we learn about Gideon in the Bible. He was hiding from the Midianites. God saw beyond Gideon's fear and focused on his faithfulness, calling Gideon a "valiant warrior" (Judges 6:12). At first Gideon pushed back by saying he was the youngest son in a weak family.

Instead of saying, "Oops, my bad," God told Gideon that He would be with him. Then God performed a sign of His power and challenged Gideon to tear down two altars to false gods. This was a scary job. The altar belonged to his father. Gideon's family would be hopping mad at him.

But Gideon obeyed. He was so scared that he carried out his mission at night to make sure nobody would see him. In the morning, two altars of evil were gone. In their place stood a shrine to the one true God.

At first, the Israelites wanted to kill Gideon. Then they realized God's hand was on him. God gave Gideon more jobs, and the people started to follow him.

Gideon became one of the first judges of Israel and a hero to the people, because he did the right thing . . . even when he was scared, even when he didn't want to, even when nobody else would . . . because he knew God was with him.

Gideon said to them, "I will not rule over you, and my son will not rule over you; the LORD will rule over you."—Judges 8:23

DEFEND YOUR FAITH

What about you? Would you like to be a hero? You don't have to win a battle against thousands. Just do what God has already made clear to you in the Bible—even if you fear you'll be teased. You can also go out of your way to treat others nicely, even those who are mean to you.

Those actions may not land your name in a Hero's Hall of Fame. But when you obey God in the small things, He'll likely give you bigger jobs, and people will start to notice. Even if you only dare do the right things when nobody is looking, you can be a hero—like Gideon.

DEFENDER FACTS

NAME: *GIDEON*

PLACE: *ISRAEL*

TIME: *ABOUT 1130 BC*

DON'T FORGET TO REMEMBER

Professional football games can be filled with high-speed highlights, bone-crushing hits, and hilarious flubs. One of the most memorable bloopers of all time was turned in by one of the greatest defensive players of all time.

In a game between the Minnesota Vikings and San Francisco 49ers on October 25, 1964, Jim Marshall made a mistake that's still remembered today. Marshall, a star defensive end for Minnesota, recovered an offensive fumble and ran 66 yards to the end zone. The problem? It was the other team's end zone. He'd run the wrong way!

Instead of scoring a touchdown for his team, Marshall put six points on the scoreboard for the 49ers. Somehow Marshall got mixed up on which direction he was supposed to go. It seems crazy that a person would actually forget something *that* important, right?

That would be like taking a canoe trip and forgetting the paddle, or being hired to mow the neighbor's lawn and forgetting the mower.

In the Bible, God talked about how ridiculous it is to forget important things, such as a bride forgetting her jewelry or her dress on her wedding day (Jeremiah 2:32).

But how much *more* important is God. He's the One who loves, protects, and creates us. Yet many people who consider themselves to be Christians can go days and days without remembering Him.

We forget to read our Bibles and hear what He has to say to us. We forget to pray and talk to God like we would a friend. We forget that God *is* God, and we do what we want to do instead of what He wants.

"Can a young woman forget her jewelry or a bride her wedding sash? Yet my people have forgotten me for countless days."
—Jeremiah 2:32

DEFEND YOUR FAITH

In the Old Testament, God's people made the biggest blunder of all time. They **abandoned** God. That means they forgot to remember Him. They broke their connection to their Creator and served false gods. They renounced their relationship with God and did what was right in their eyes. Abandoning God doesn't happen overnight. It can happen gradually. We get busy and put other priorities above God.

People have joked about football superstar Jim Marshall forgetting which way to run, but often we forget which way we should be going in our everyday lives. Be sure not to forget to remember God every day. If we're not running toward Him, we're going the wrong way.

A MESSAGE TO
MESSED-UP PEOPLE

There are basically two kinds of Christians—at least when it comes to how we treat people who are "messed up." (Hint: In reality, we're *all* messed up.)

> • Judgers are quick to point out a person's sin. They use the Bible to show how wrong the sinner is.
> • Huggers are quick to love people who are sinning. They accept them for who they are.

Judgers and Huggers are usually convinced they're treating "sinners" right. But which way is the best way to treat people who are making bad decisions in their lives?

To find out, look at how Jesus treated sinners. John 8:1–11 tells the story of some religious leaders who were classic Judgers. A woman had sinned terribly, and they knew God's Word said she deserved to be punished. They took her in front of Jesus to get His opinion of what should be done.

Jesus didn't answer right away. He stooped down and wrote on the ground with his finger. Then He stood up and said, "The one without sin among you should be the first to throw a stone at her" (John 8:7). With those words, Jesus bent down and continued writing on the ground.

What did He write? Nobody knows. Bible experts have a lot of guesses. Maybe Jesus wrote the sins that those leaders had committed. Things like pride, selfishness, dishonesty, and jealousy. Others think Jesus wrote the names of each of the accusers.

No matter what Jesus wrote, it caused the Judgers to leave until nobody was left to punish the woman. Then Jesus told the women not to sin anymore.

Many Bible scholars don't believe John originally recorded the story of the woman and the religious leaders in his gospel. Maybe you have a footnote in your Bible that says that. They think it was added later. Nonetheless, people agree that the story does line up perfectly with how Jesus treated sinners.

"Go, and from now on do not sin anymore."
—John 8:11

Defend Your Faith

Jesus didn't condemn the woman. He saved her, telling her that she had to live differently in the future. Here and in other places in the Bible, Jesus didn't simply "accept" sinners and overlook their sin. Jesus loved and met people where they were—for the purpose of saving them and changing them.

- Judgers often fail to love sinners.
- Huggers often fail to tell sinners that they can't stay as they are and must be saved.

Jesus shows us the better way. When we see people making bad decisions, we can be like Jesus. First, love them. Second, tell them the truth that it's not okay to live in sin. They need Jesus to save them and help them to change.

HOW CAN I HELP A HURTING FRIEND?

God is *always* good, but bad things happen in this world. Sickness, tornados, pandemics, bike accidents, and other bad news can affect our lives and the lives of our friends. When we see a friend who's hurting, we naturally want to help. But we often don't know what to say.

Saying something like, "If there's anything I can do to help, let me know," makes *us* feel better. But rarely will a hurting person actually tell us how to help. Most of the time they're feeling so weak, defeated, or scared that they don't know what to ask.

In the Bible, Jonathan often helped his best friend, David, when he was hurting or facing hard times. Jonathan is the kind of friend most people wish they had. He saw when David was hurting. He pointed David to God. And he saved David's life.

When David was running for his life, Jonathan told him, "Don't be afraid" (1 Samuel 23:16–17). King Saul wanted to kill David. David had gone from future king to fugitive. His world had been turned upside down.

Read the verses on the next page, and notice these two principles Jonathan used to help hurting friends.

1. Don't wait for them to come to you. Go to them instead.
2. Encourage your friend's faith in God.

God can help your friend in more ways than you ever could. Some Bibles translate this verse as Jonathan helping David "find strength in God." But how do you do that? One of the best ways is to focus on God's power—instead of what's making them feel weak, scared, or defeated. God is in control. His plans can't be stopped (Psalm 33:10–11).

Saul's son Jonathan came to David in Horesh and encouraged him in his faith in God, saying, "Don't be afraid."—1 Samuel 23:16–17

Defend Your Faith

Jonathan didn't come to David and say, "Hey, you've got this." Jonathan didn't give David a pep talk. He gave him a God talk. He reminded David of God's plan and God's power.

Did Jonathan help his friend? Yes. And you can help someone who's hurting in similar ways. Don't wait for them to come to you. Go to them where they are, and encourage their faith in God. Remind them that God's love for them never changes (Romans 8:35–39), that God will never leave them (Hebrews 13:5–6), and that God works out impossible things for their good (Romans 8:28). When you help your friends find their strength in God, you'll be the kind of friend everybody wishes they had.

THE BEST ADVICE

Imagine you've got a big decision to make. You ask some people for advice. Parents. Grandparents. Friends. Maybe an older brother or sister. These people likely have different opinions on what you should do. So how do you know which advice to follow?

In 1 Kings 12, it tells what happened to King Rehoboam when he needed help with a big decision. Rehoboam had just taken the throne after King Solomon died. Solomon had turned away from God later in his life and treated the people harshly. The people in his kingdom were tired. They wanted the new king to make life easier for them. Rehoboam asked the people for three days to get advice and make his decision. Then he met with two groups:

• **The Elders.** These men were older than Rehoboam and had years of experience as leaders. They advised Rehoboam to speak nicely to the people, treat them with kindness, and serve the people as a good leader should.

• **His Friends.** These were guys Rehoboam grew up with. They didn't have much experience leading, but they had lots of opinions. They advised Rehoboam to be harder on the people than his father was as king. They encouraged Rehoboam to talk tough and make the people afraid of him.

King Rehoboam took the advice of his friends. He was proud and harsh. And he made a big mistake. When the people heard Rehoboam's answer, they rebelled against the king, and Rehoboam lost most of his kingdom.

Arrogance leads to nothing but strife, but
wisdom is gained by those who take advice.
—Proverbs 13:10

Defend Your Faith

Rehoboam listened to the wrong advice. To recognize good advice and make good decisions, follow these tips:

1. Listen carefully to older people, like parents and grandparents. They are likely to give you better advice than friends.

2. Make sure the advice agrees with God's Word. The advice Rehoboam got from the Elders fit perfectly with what the Bible says: leaders should be servants—not tyrants. The advice from his friends was selfish and greedy.

3. Pray. Rehoboam did not ask God to lead him. Prayers let you focus more on God and His will.

You will have to make big decisions in life. Don't rush. Rehoboam was wise to take time to think and get advice. But he was foolish to act selfishly. When you listen to godly people, line up your plan with the Bible, and pray for wisdom, you'll make great decisions—not a royal mess!

Defamer Facts
Name: *King Rehoboam*
Place: *Israel*
Time: *About 970 bc*

WHAT A KISS AND HONESTY HAVE IN COMMON

Wait a sec, you might be thinking. *Are we going to be talking about kissing here?* Yes, but before you flip the page, take a look at this verse from Proverbs 24:26: "He who gives an honest answer gives a kiss on the lips."

What is *that* all about? Back in Bible days, people didn't shake hands when they were greeting each other. They gave the other person a kiss on the cheek or lips. Some cultures still greet each other that way.

You probably shake hands, hug, or give an elbow bump for a greeting. But several times in the New Testament, it tells Christ followers to greet each other with a "holy kiss." This kiss was a sign of connection and respect.

But there are other types of kisses. When two people kiss on the lips—like maybe you see your parents do—it's a demonstration of love and commitment.

Going back to the verse, if an honest answer is like a kiss on the lips and a kiss on the lips is a mark of love, respect, connection, and commitment, then an honest answer is a demonstration of love, respect, connection, and commitment too.

Being honest is a loving thing to do. That's why your parents get so hurt if you lie to them. When you love and respect someone, you demonstrate that by telling the truth.

The word **honesty** doesn't appear that many times in the Bible. Being honest means you speak the truth. But it also has a deeper meaning of acting honorably. Honesty is a condition of the heart, where you're truthful and sincere.

So does that mean we are required to be brutally honest with people? Let's say your brother or sister does poorly on a test. Is it okay to say, "Wow, you're really dumb"? Definitely not. Being honest is not an excuse to be rude. We are to tell the truth in a loving way and "do everything in love" (1 Corinthians

16:14). So it's much better to say to a hurting sibling, "History is hard. I can help you study next time if you'd like."

Putting away lying, speak the truth, each one to his neighbor, because we are members of one another.—Ephesians 4:25

DEFEND YOUR FAITH

Although you won't find a lot of verses about honesty in God's Word, you will find a lot of verses about not lying and watching the words that come out of your mouth.

You love your parents, right? You love God too. If you want to show how much you care, remember that an honest answer is a sign of love. Then do the loving thing. Tell the truth—not half-truths—to your parents, to your friends and family, and to God.

TRUTH FROM THE TRASH

For hundreds of years, people who doubt the Bible have said, "The book of Genesis isn't true!" These skeptics say Genesis is filled with stories of people and events that never happened. But again and again as archaeologists dig up artifacts in the Holy Land, they uncover evidence that shows Genesis is accurate.

Until recently, historical scholars thought the nation of Edom came into existence around 850 BC. The biblical account shows the first king of Israel (Saul) was crowned around 1021 BC. So is Genesis 36:31 wrong when it claims there were kings in Edom "before any king reigned over the Israelites"? Of course not.

In 2019, a team of researchers dug through ancient garbage that was found in the southern deserts of Israel and Jordan. According to the Bible, this was once a stronghold of the Edomite kingdom. The kingdom of Edom was founded by Esau, Jacob's brother (Genesis 36:9). The Edomites lived in an extremely rugged land. They chiseled cities in the face of cliffs so enemy armies would have a hard time attacking them (Obadiah 1:1–3).

The team of archaeologists from the United States, Israel, and Jordan found evidence of copper production in the ancient waste. This metal "garbage" proved that the Edomites were mining copper and building their cities around 1050 BC—three hundred years before some scholars originally thought and well before Saul became king. This new, correct date totally matches the Bible's account.

God's Word contains more truth than just the fact of when the Edomites existed. Every word is true, including the way He lifts out treasure from the trash.

He raises the poor from the dust and lifts the needy from the trash heap. He seats them with noblemen and gives them a throne of honor.—1 Samuel 2:8

DEFEND YOUR FAITH

Finding treasure in the trash may seem surprising, but God does it all the time. He takes people who have been forgotten by society and lifts them up. God doesn't want us to ignore the poor, just like the researchers didn't ignore the trash. When we help the less fortunate, Jesus says it's like we're helping Him (Matthew 25:40).

Countless stories exist of kids making a difference in the lives of the needy. Four siblings in Portland, Oregon, handed out thousands of sleeping bags to the homeless over the course of a decade. Another boy in Georgia sold pickles and raised nearly $100,000 to gives homes to the homeless.

You can help too. Maybe you can gather bottled water, granola bars, tissues, Bibles, and socks. Keep them in the car to give to people on the side of the road. Your family could help a local ministry that serves the poor. You can also remember the poor in your prayers, asking God to keep them safe.

THE HOLY LAND

What comes to mind when you hear the words *Holy Land*? Maybe you picture a land of holes, such as a prairie dog town filled with burrows and tunnels. The world's largest prairie dog town was located in Texas and covered 25,000 square miles. That's the size of West Virginia. It's estimated that 400 million prairie dogs lived in this thriving community.

Although that would certainly be a "holey land," it's not the Holy Land where the events in the Bible took place. The first families mentioned in Genesis formed nations in the areas now known as the Middle East and Western Asia. Bible experts still don't know exactly where the Garden of Eden was located, but God's Word mentions four rivers in the garden, including the Tigris and Euphrates (Genesis 2:10–14). Today, these rivers flow through parts of Turkey, Syria, Iraq, Iran, and Kuwait.

The *Promised Land*, where Moses led God's people, is referred to as Canaan. That area now includes the countries of Israel, Jordan, Syria, and Lebanon. And you probably know that the Israelites were slaves in Egypt (Northern Africa) before God sent Moses to set them free.

Egypt is also the place where Jesus' parents took Him to keep Him safe from King Herod. The Bible explains that Herod wanted to kill Jesus because he was afraid the Child would grow up to be an earthly king and take over his kingdom. But Jesus was the King of kings, not an earthly king. After King Herod died, Jesus' parents took Him back to Israel, and He grew up in Nazareth.

As you read the Bible, if you don't know where a place is, check it out on a map, like the ones at the back of the *Defend Your Faith Bible*. Look up cities like Bethlehem, Jerusalem, and Rome. Find the Sea of Galilee, the Jordan

River, the Tigris and Euphrates rivers, and other Bible locations. They're all there, and they're all real.

"If anyone serves me, he must follow me. Where I am, there my servant also will be. If anyone serves me, the Father will honor him."
—John 12:26

DEFEND YOUR FAITH

Jesus traveled the Holy Land without a GPS, smartphone, bike, or car. Sometimes He rode in a boat on the Sea of Galilee. But usually He walked. Some Bible experts estimate Jesus walked at least three thousand miles during the three years of His ministry.

During that same time, the Gospel writers record Jesus saying "Follow Me" more than twenty times. The disciples literally followed Jesus as He walked to spread the good news of God's forgiveness. Even today, Jesus calls you to follow Him. You may not be able to walk with Him through the Holy Land. But you can follow Him by acting, talking, and living in a holy way that honors Him.

BIBLICAL NAME-CALLING

Do you know why your parents chose the name they gave you? You should ask sometime. Parents often choose names of close family members, friends, or characters they love from books, movies, and TV shows. Aren't you glad your parents didn't choose a name from a favorite Disney movie, such as *Dumbo* or *Maleficent*?

Parents in Bible times also chose names that had a special meaning. In the Old Testament, you'll find many names that end in *el*, like Samuel or Ezekiel. That's because *El* means god. Lots of Old Testament names also end in *ah*, like Hezekiah or Jeremiah. *Ah* is the last part of another one of God's names—*Jehovah*.

Names in the New Testament had special meanings too. Look at John the Baptist's parents. Considering that John was the person who announced the coming of Jesus, they had very interesting names.

The last promise God made in the Old Testament stated He would send a person like the prophet Elijah (notice the *El* and the *ah* in his name) to prepare the people for the day of the LORD (see Malachi 4:5–6). Four hundred years later, an angel announced to John's father that his son would be a special messenger (see Luke 1:16–17). Many Bible experts believe John was the fulfillment of God's last promise in the Old Testament.

John's father was named Zechariah (*ah*) and his mother was named Elizabeth (*el*). Zechariah means *God remembers*. Elizabeth means *promise of God*. Put that together, and John the Baptist's parents have names that mean *God remembers His promise*!

*God highly exalted him and gave him the
name that is above every name, so that at
the name of Jesus every knee will bow.
—Philippians 2:9–10*

DEFEND YOUR FAITH

Jesus was God's promise. He came to rescue sinful people and restore our relationship with God. The Bible cites dozens of names for Jesus. In Isaiah 9:6, Jesus is called "Wonderful Counselor, Mighty God, Eternal Father, Prince of Peace."

All of these names can be confusing. Some people might say, "So what is it? Is Jesus the Lamb of God, a strong tower, or the Lion of Judah? He can't be all of those because some are opposites."

But Jesus embodies all those names and more! Jesus can't be summarized by a single name. He existed before the beginning of time, came to earth in human form, died on a cross, rose from the dead, and is coming in the future as a conquering king. We'll never fully know everything about Jesus, but studying His names helps.

As you read the Bible, look for the different names of Jesus. You can learn something from each one. And you can start with *Jesus*. It means *Jehovah saves.*

HOW HIGH ARE THE HEAVENS?

Do you know how big the universe is? The answer is . . . no.

Do scientists even know the size of the universe? Again, the answer is no. Scientists can *estimate* how big the universe is. Some astronomers say the farthest known object is 13.7 billion light years away from earth. That means if you could get in a car and drive at the speed of light—about 186,000 miles per *second*—it would take you thirteen billion years to get there. Now factor in the distance light travels in one year is 5.88 trillion miles and multiple by 13 billion, and that's a really looooooong way!

God created the heavens and everything in them. He placed all the planets and stars in the universe and stretched out the universe so that everything constantly moves away from us.

Scientists have made some amazing discoveries about the universe. They believe we can see only about five percent of the stuff God created. The other ninety-five percent of matter is not visible to the human eye.

Will science ever be able to explain all the mysteries of the universe? You know the answer. No! Our minds will never comprehend the majesty, magnificence, and magnitude of God's creation.

The edge of the universe is so far away that God uses it to illustrate some very important truths about Himself. In Psalm 103, God uses the heights of the heavens as a measure for how much He loves His children. In Isaiah 55:9, God says the heights of the heavens are an example of how much higher His wisdom and abilities are above ours.

So why does God use the heights of the heavens to characterize His love and wisdom? After all, we could never measure it or even understand it.

That's exactly God's point! He is so much wiser than we are and loves His people so much that we could never fully comprehend that kind of wisdom and love.

As high as the heavens are above the earth, so great is his faithful love toward those who fear him.—Psalm 103:11

DEFEND YOUR FAITH

God also uses the size of the heavens in an interesting way in Jeremiah 31:37. That verse says if we are able to measure the distance of the heavens, then God will take back His promise to always love and protect the people of Israel. Of course, God never goes back on His word, so that means we will *never* be able to accurately measure the size of His universe. His promise depends on it!

If there's one thing you can depend on, it's the promises of God. He always keeps His word. Think about that the next time you look up into the night sky.

THINK ABOUT WHAT YOU THINK ABOUT

What do you think about during the day? Do you plan what you'll do after school or over the weekend? Do you dream about what you want to be when you grow up? Do you remember past failures and embarrassments? Do you picture the places you'd like to travel to?

Think about the one thing that comes to your mind the most every day. When you keep thinking about the same thing and mentally map out the steps to make this thought come true, you're doing what the Bible calls *meditation*.

Meditation means to think about something over and over. You focus your mind on it and think deeply about it so that you can decide what to do next. What you mediate on can influence your mood and what you accomplish in life. That's why God wants you to meditate on His Word to help you make right decisions in life.

Meditation is a big part of many religions. But many of these religions want you to "empty" your mind, think about nothing, and find inner peace. God doesn't want you to empty your mind. He wants you to fill it up with Jesus!

Have you ever heard the saying about "seeing the world through rose-colored glasses"? It means you have a "rosy" view of life where everything is happy and nice. That's not always reality. God wants us to be real. He encourages us to view His universe through "Jesus-colored" glasses so we can see Him working all around us.

How happy is the one who does not walk in the advice of the wicked or stand in the pathway with sinners. . . . Instead, his delight is in the LORD's instruction, and he meditates on it day and night.—Psalm 1:1–2

DEFEND YOUR FAITH

When we meditate on His Word day and night, we can know what to do in every situation. As the Bible fills our brains, we look at nature and see God's fingerprints in everything— from gophers to galaxies. When we put on "Jesus-colored" glasses, we see our lives from His perspective and know that He is at work every minute of every day. If instead we listen to bad advice, think about inappropriate song lyrics, or dwell on selfish dreams, it can take us down a destructive path.

Our thoughts control our actions and influence our decisions. Focusing our thoughts on God and the wisdom of His Word leads us to success (Joshua 1:8). So meditate day and night, and see your life through God's eyes.

PATH THROUGH THE SEA

What would you think if a friend told you that next Thursday you'd have a substitute teacher with blonde hair and glasses who spoke with a French accent and gave you homework that required frozen fish? Crazy, right? But what if that was exactly what happened? Would you listen to your friend more closely the next time he predicted something in the future?

The Bible identifies many men and women whom God gave knowledge of future events. They're called *prophets*. Through God's inspiration, these prophets made hundreds of prophecies that came true in amazing detail.

One of the most interesting is a prophecy about the ancient city of Tyre. God's prophet Ezekiel predicted the city would be completely destroyed because the people rejected God and practiced evil. At the time, Tyre was one of the most powerful cities in the world. Nobody would've thought it could be brought to ruins. But Ezekiel said even the stones, wood, and dirt of the city would be thrown into the water (Ezekiel 26:12).

Soon after Ezekiel gave his prophecy, the city was attacked for thirteen years by the army of Babylon. Babylon finally defeated Tyre and left it in ruins. Some people escaped to an island offshore and built another strong city. Nearly 250 years later, Alexander the Great conquered that island city by building a half-mile-long path through the water. History shows that Alexander's armies created the "path" by throwing all the rocks, lumber, and dirt from the original site of Tyre into the sea. More recent geologic studies of the area show that the island was linked to the land by a stretch of sand that was about ten feet below the water. That made it a bit easier for Alexander to build the path and conquer the last remnants of Tyre.

The entirety of your word is truth, each
of your righteous judgments endures forever.
—Psalm 119:160

DEFEND YOUR FAITH

Ezekiel's prophecy was fulfilled in amazing detail because God knew what would happen to Tyre and its people. In fact, this prophecy came true with such accuracy that some people claimed that the book of Ezekiel was written after Tyre was destroyed. But Ezekiel lived and prophesied nearly three hundred years *before* Alexander the Great attacked Tyre in 332 BC.

The Bible is full of prophecies like this. At the time many prophecies were made, people didn't believe they could come true. But they did. All of God's Word is true. We can always trust what we read in the Bible . . . even when it seems impossible.

GOOD NEWS FOR
BAD NEWS PEOPLE

When you think of Vikings, you may picture pirating, pillaging, and plundering. That's only part of the picture. One of the most famous Vikings was also a powerful promoter of God's truth.

Leif Eriksson is best known for his sea voyages. Around the year 1000, he sailed from Greenland to North America, probably landing on what is now Newfoundland (get it—New Found Land), an island off eastern Canada. But before he found a new land, Leif brought "new life" to Greenland.

Leif was one of Erik the Red's four children. Erik was a classic Viking. His father was banished from Norway for murder. Then Erik was banished from Iceland for killing. He founded a Viking colony on Greenland, more than 800 miles across the ocean.

As a young man, Erik's son Leif became an expert navigator and ship captain. During a trip to trade goods with Norway, Leif gained an audience with the king. The king was a Christian and asked Leif to be his ambassador, bringing the gospel message to the Vikings in Greenland.

Leif believed in the truth of Jesus. Many people on Greenland became Christians because of Leif's testimony. Leif's mother even joyfully accepted the gift of salvation and built a church.

We are ambassadors for Christ, since God is making his appeal through us. We plead on Christ's behalf: "Be reconciled to God."
—2 Corinthians 5:20

DEFEND YOUR FAITH

If you think telling your friends about Jesus is tough, think of what Leif Eriksson had to go through. He was sharing a message of forgiveness and love to a violent society. These people solved their quarrels through revenge and savagery. Even his grandfather and his father were men used to seeking vengeance on their own terms.

Leif chose a different way, a peaceful way. Not everyone followed Jesus, but many did. God calls you to be His ambassador. You can't make anyone believe. That's the Holy Spirit's job. But you can do your part by telling others about Jesus and what He's done in your life—even people you think are the least likely to believe it.

DEFENDER FACTS
NAME: *LEIF ERIKSSON*
PLACE: *GREENLAND*
TIME: *970–1020*

PRAYER IS A BALANCING ACT

Nik Wallenda earned his title "King of the High Wire" by doing what seemed impossible. He walked across a tightrope above Niagara Falls, an active volcano, and even the Grand Canyon. Then he went a step further and tightroped between two skyscrapers in Chicago—blindfolded! He battled high winds, high heat, and high altitudes to do what had never been done before.

At times TV cameras captured Nik praying aloud as he took each step. But what if Nik stopped halfway across the thin wire—and stayed there to pray—instead of moving forward? He wouldn't have completed his mission.

In the Bible, Moses did what seemed impossible. He talked with God and led the Israelites out of Egypt. But when he got to the Red Sea, Pharaoh's army had him trapped. The terrified people blamed Moses and cried out to God. Moses told them to stand firm and be still—God would rescue them.

Moses must have prayed too, because in Exodus 14:15 God asked why he was crying out to Him. God didn't want Moses to keep praying and praying. In this case, Moses needed to get moving and get the people across the Red Sea.

But why would God tell Moses to stop praying, and then later tell His people to "pray constantly" (1 Thessalonians 5:16–18). That doesn't seem to fit together.

Sometimes Christ followers can get stuck in an "I'll pray about it" mode. Prayer is good, and God wants us to constantly be talking to Him. But there are times when God has already impressed on our hearts what we're to do—but we stall, using the excuse that we're praying.

When the Israelites were "trapped" at the Red Sea, God was ready to act. He had led the people to that exact place to perform a miracle. Now Moses needed to move forward.

Rejoice always, pray constantly, give thanks in everything; for this is God's will for you in Christ Jesus.—1 Thessalonians 5:16–18

DEFEND YOUR FAITH

Scripture records Moses praying after the people were safe on the other side of the Red Sea. So was God suggesting prayer wasn't needed in Exodus 14:15? No. But Moses wasn't to use prayer as a reason not to step out in faith.

That's a good lesson for us too. Prayer is essential, but we must be careful not to use it as an excuse not to move forward. When we pray for God's help or direction—and we get a clear indication of what we should do—we need to act.

That doesn't mean we stop praying. Like Moses, we should pray before and after a task is complete. Like Nik Wallenda, we should pray as we go. Prayer is a balancing act. Pray constantly, but don't get stuck when God is ready to show His power and wants you to move.

WHAT'S WRONG WITH BEING PROUD?

If you heat up a marshmallow too long in a microwave, it will grow freakishly huge, turn brown, and burst into flame. Warning: Don't try this at home; your parents won't be happy.

As people, we can get puffed up too. But instead of being destroyed by absorbing heat energy, we destroy ourselves by becoming proud. Pride comes when we absorb the praise we get—without giving God credit.

In Acts 12 the Bible tells of King Herod's death. This king was a really bad guy. He'd arrested the apostle Peter and had Jesus' brother James killed. Just before Herod died, he got mad at the people in the towns of Tyre and Sidon. The people were afraid, because they depended on the food that came from the king's country. These towns wanted to get on King Herod's good side, hoping he would be kind to them. So when the king gave a speech, the crowds shouted, "It's the voice of a god, not of a man!"

Instead of trying to stop the people from calling him a god, Herod absorbed the praise—like a marshmallow in a microwave. He got puffed up with pride. The king was so self-centered that he actually believed it. That was Herod's final and fatal mistake. God dealt with him immediately. The angel of the Lord struck Herod dead, and the wicked king was eaten by worms.

King Herod's story illustrates the incredible danger of pride. The king wanted the people to praise him. He wanted to be lifted up and seen as powerful. He was arrogant.

Obviously, that's a problem. But what about taking pride in your work? Isn't it okay to feel good when your parents, a teacher, or a coach says, "You did a great job; you should be proud of yourself"?

Having a feeling of accomplishment, especially after reaching a goal or succeeding in school or sports, is a good thing. We can be proud of working on a talent and seeing it pay off. But if we simply absorb praise without giving God credit, we open ourselves up to becoming proud.

Pride comes before destruction, and an arrogant spirit before a fall.—Proverbs 16:18

DEFEND YOUR FAITH

To help prevent yourself from getting a feeling of superiority, answer these questions.

1. Who gave you your ability?
2. Who gave you the opportunity?

Then be sure to quickly pass the praise to the ones who really deserve it: God, your parents, teammates, teachers, and coaches. When you show gratefulness to the people around you, it keeps you from becoming proud. Do that, and you won't end up like a microwaved marshmallow—all puffed up and messed up.

ROCK ON

Would you rather play volleyball on a sandy beach or on a big rock? It's definitely more fun to dive in the sand than smash your knees on a rock.

Scientifically, rock and sand are basically the same material. Sand is just *pulverized* rock that's been broken down into tiny pieces. If you look closely at sand, you'll find bits of rock, shells, and sea life. Sand can be different colors depending on where it's found in the world. In Hawaii, where there's lots of volcanic rock, the sand can be black because that's the color of the rock it's made from.

In one of Jesus' most famous talks called the Sermon on the Mount, He pointed out there's a huge difference between sand and rock. Jesus told the large crowd that people who heard His words would fall into two groups. One group would be like a homeowner who built a new house on sand. These people were the ones who heard God's Word but didn't act on it. However, those who believed and obeyed His words were like a homeowner who built a new house on solid rock.

Jesus explained when storms hit—and they always do— that the house built on sand collapsed with a great crash because its foundation washed away. But the house built on rock didn't budge. Its foundation didn't shift at all.

God's wisdom is like a solid rock you can always depend on. The truth in the Bible doesn't change. What was true two thousand years ago is still true today. Popular ideas, on the other hand, shift. Some people believe amassing wealth is the only purpose in life. But what happens when their money disappears or their businesses close? If you build your life on anything but God, it's like having a foundation on sand that shifts and blows away.

"Everyone who hears these words of mine and acts on them will be like a wise man who built his house on the rock."—Matthew 7:24

DEFEND YOUR FAITH

Think about what happens when you step on sand. Your feet sink in. But what happens when you step barefoot on hard rock? The bottom of your foot takes on some of the shape of the rock. Jesus knows when we trust and obey Him that His solid Word "shapes" our thinking and our lives. We conform and become more like Him.

Building your life by following Jesus makes good scientific, engineering sense. It gives you a strong foundation. It also helps you choose good friends, make right decisions, learn good habits, and be a person others will trust and listen to. Then you can help your friends step out of the sand and onto the Rock.

SHOW A LITTLE (OR A LOT) OF RESPECT

Old people have lived a lot of years. That's a fact nobody can argue with.

The Bible is full of amazing stories of old people. Methuselah lived 969 years. His grandson, Noah, lived to be 950. Noah was six hundred years old when the earth was flooded. That means he was building the ark when he was over five hundred!

Sometimes we may see older people as being not all that important. Some dress funny, have hearing problems, and are really bad with figuring out technology. Many older people seem forgotten by their families.

God doesn't forget older people—or any people—ever. We're all important to Him and deserve respect. In 2 Kings 2, there's a bizarre story of a group of boys mocking a special servant of God named Elisha. They jeered at him, calling him "Baldy." Baldness was seen as a weakness. These boys didn't show Elisha respect as a man of God or as someone who was older.

Elisha looked at the children and asked God to deal with them. Immediately, two bears stormed out of the woods and mauled forty-two of the youths. Not a pretty picture. God sent a very hard message to those children. Older people deserve respect, not ridicule.

Elisha may not have looked special, but he was a great man in God's eyes. Those kids would've been better off asking for his autograph instead of belittling his baldness. Our world is showing less and less respect to older people. Don't be part of that. Christians are called to be different . . . and respecting older people is one way you can stand out.

"You are to rise in the presence of the elderly and honor the old. Fear your God; I am the LORD."—Leviticus 19:32

DEFEND YOUR FAITH

Honoring older people is practically a lost art. We might rush by them in a store or not look forward to visiting older relatives during family get-togethers. If you want to show respect to those older than you, try these ideas.

• **Check your attitude**. Older people may walk with a limp or not have the abilities or energy they once had. But they've handled the worst life can dish out—and they've survived. That definitely earns some respect. Instead of dismissing older people, find out their secrets for succeeding in life.

• **Talk to older people**. Grandparents and great-aunts and great-uncles love when you hang out with them. Seek their advice. Ask what they enjoyed when they were younger. Often their insights and experience can help you.

• **Do something nice**. Clean up an elder neighbor's yard. Help with a project at a retirement home. Write a card or create a drawing for your grandparents.

PUZZLING PARABLES

Jesus often taught in stories called *parables*. His parables were based on everyday events that people in the crowd could relate to. Although the people all recognized the real-life situations, not everyone understood the deeper meaning of Jesus' teaching—like in the two short parables He shared in Matthew 13:44–46.

In the first parable, Jesus told of a man who found a treasure buried in a field. The man joyfully sold everything he had and bought the field to win the treasure. In the second parable, Jesus told a story of a merchant searching for pearls. Once the man found a priceless pearl, he sold all his possessions and bought it.

After reading these stories, you probably picture yourself as the man or the merchant. That's exactly what Jesus was hoping. He wants us to imagine that we're the person who discovered the treasure or the pearl, because we *can*! The "treasures" Jesus talked about really represent eternal life in heaven. In the parables, the men *sold* all they had and *bought* the pearl or the field with the treasure because it was the most important thing they could ever do.

Wait a sec, you might be thinking. *Isn't the Bible clear that we can't buy our way into heaven? So what was Jesus' real meaning behind these stories?*

Jesus never contradicted the Bible with His words. As the ultimate author of every word in the Bible, He couldn't say anything that contradicted the Word because He can't contradict Himself. (Pause to think about that for a while.)

The point of these parables is that we must be willing to give up everything for God. Jesus makes that clear in what He said right after these parables. He compared the kingdom of heaven to a net that collected fish in the sea. Only the good ones were kept (see Matthew 13:47–50).

For you are saved by grace through faith, and this is not for yourselves; it is God's gift—not from works, so that no one can boast.
—Ephesians 2:8–9

DEFEND YOUR FAITH

Nobody can buy his or her way into God's kingdom. It's a gift from God when we believe in Him and put our faith in the truth of His Word (Ephesians 2:8–9). The point of these parables is that the kingdom of heaven is worth sacrificing every worldly possession and advantage we have. The rich young ruler discovered this in Mark 10:17–22, but he wasn't willing to give up his wealth and walked away from having eternal life.

God wants us to choose His unique and valuable treasure of salvation over anything the world offers. When we willingly give up everything for God, we become citizens of God's kingdom and gain the ultimate prize.

Suddenly those parables aren't so puzzling after all!

HOW DO YOU HONOR YOUR PARENTS?

Who's your hero? You know, the person you look up to most.

Goliath probably isn't the best answer, even though he was nine feet tall.

In surveys, some kids choose athletes, doctors, singers, or movie stars as their heroes. Maybe you thought of Jesus or another person from the Bible. But when a majority of people think of their hero, they picture their mom or dad.

Although parents are the most popular pick as heroes, many kids don't treat them that way. Instead of obeying right away and not complaining when our parents ask us to do something, we pretend we didn't hear them or start whining. We ignore "house rules" that our parents set—like limiting screen time or doing homework before playing—and do what we want to do instead.

Obviously, that's not honoring. Simply put, you honor your parents by valuing them and treating them with respect because God has put them in charge of you.

Your parents may treat you like a prince or princess, but remember . . . they're the king and queen! They deserve honor because they provide, protect, and love you. You can show honor in many ways:

- Paying attention when parents talk to you.
- Making their lives easier—rather than expecting them to constantly serve you.
- Respectfully talking to—and about—them.
- Speaking and behaving in ways that would make them proud, even if they aren't around.
- Becoming the kind of person they've taught you to be.

Children, obey your parents in the Lord,
because this is right. Honor your father and
mother, which is the first commandment with
a promise, so that it may go well with you and
that you may have a long life in the land.
—Ephesians 6:1–3

DEFEND YOUR FAITH

After reading the list on the previous page, you probably noticed that many of your friends don't treat their parents in those ways. Jesus calls you to a higher standard. He expects you to honor your parents throughout your entire life. It's just one of the ways you can be an example as a Christ follower.

It's also a secret way you have to living a better life. Read the last part of Ephesians 6:1–3 again. Many of God's commands don't come with a promise, but this one does . . . and it's a pretty good one. Honoring Dad and Mom is so important that God promises us a better life if we do. Wow—who doesn't want that!? So try it. Do what the Bible says, and treat your parents like the heroes they are.

¿Habla usted Ingles?

Sprechen Sie Englisch?

Parlez-vous anglais?

Eigo ga hanasemasu ka?

Did you understand that? All those sentences say the same thing: *Do you speak English?* But one is in Spanish, one is German, one is French, and one is Japanese.

Have you ever wondered why there are so many languages in the world? Wouldn't it be easier to communicate if everyone spoke the same language?

Yes, it would. And God created the world that way. Everyone on the planet spoke one language until a few decades after Noah's ark survived the great flood. Then people started making better technology (see Genesis 11:1–9). Back then it was bricks, not smartphones. They decided to build a great city with a tower that reached the sky. Instead of worshipping the Creator of the stars and sun, they started to worship the stars and sun. The people were proud of their accomplishments, putting themselves on a pedestal and rejecting the God of Noah.

Because the people disobeyed God's commands, the Lord did something He knew would stop their rebellion and cause them to spread out over the earth. He caused groups of people to speak in different languages.

Suddenly, when one worker said to another, "Hand me the hammer," the other man couldn't understand him. That stopped the building project. The people formed new groups based on who they could understand. Those who spoke the same new language started hanging out. Eventually these groups moved away from the city, leaving the tower unfinished.

This city became known as Babylon, based on the word *babel*, which means "confusion." When God confused the people's language, He helped create all the different nations around the world.

"I will then restore pure speech to the peoples so that all of them may call on the name of the LORD."—Zephaniah 3:9

DEFEND YOUR FAITH

God created the world with one language, and He'll again give all the people pure speech when He creates a new heaven and a new earth (see Revelation 21:1–4). Many of God's prophets wrote about a time when God would return and make things perfect again. Nobody knows exactly when that time will come. Jesus said the angels—and even He—didn't know the exact hour (Matthew 24:36). But until then, God wants us to be ready and to battle against babel.

There's nothing confusing about following God. He tells us to love God and to love others. The best way we can love other people is to share with them the good news that salvation can be found only in Jesus. People translate the Bible into different languages and travel the world to spread God's truth. You can do your part by talking about Jesus with those who speak your language.

In Victorian England, much like today, many women found it easy to fall in love with rich, handsome men. But in 1856, Susannah Thompson married Charles Spurgeon, a young Baptist preacher. He wasn't rich. He wasn't handsome. But Charles challenged Susie (that's what her friends called her) to read the Bible more, and that made him easy to love. Susie knew if she married Charles, she would grow closer to God. That's what she wanted more than anything else.

Many other people wanted to grow closer to God through Charles's teaching from God's Word. He quickly became one of the most popular pastors in London. But not everyone could hear Charles preach because there was no radio or TV.

To solve the problem, Charles wrote down his sermons and published a book called *Lectures to My Students*. As soon as Susie read it, she told her husband that she wished every minister in England could have a copy. But in those days, pastors were painfully poor. Most of them struggled to pay for food and medicine for their children. They didn't have extra money to buy books.

"Why don't you pay for the books?" Charles told her. "How much will you give?"

On that day in 1875, Susie went to her room and counted the money she'd been saving. She discovered that she had enough to pay for one hundred copies of the book. Then she asked other people to donate to the Book Fund (that's what she called it). By the time she died in 1903, Susie had put more than 200,000 of Charles's books into pastors' hands.

If anyone has this world's goods and sees a fellow believer in need but withholds compassion from him—how does God's love reside in him?—1 John 3:17

DEFEND YOUR FAITH

Susie's legacy lives on through the Susannah Project that puts biblical training materials into the hands of pastors all over the world. Stop and think about how many lives Susie impacted for Christ.

And what did she do? She saw a need and she met it. Susie knew other pastors needed training in God's Word to be effective in their ministry.

When you look around, what needs do you see? Do you know a kid at school who always wears the same clothes? Do you see a neighbor who can't keep up with their yardwork? You can use your time wisely by meeting a need of a neighbor or family member. You can also be like Susie and give away some of your money to spread God's truth.

It's easy to notice the rich and attractive. Look deeper to see the needs of the less noticeable people who live around you.

DEFENDER FACTS
NAME: *SUSANNAH SPURGEON*
PLACE: *LONDON, ENGLAND*
TIME: *1832–1903*

BUBBLE, BUBBLE LEADS TO TROUBLE

Think of things that bubble.

- Soap bubbles when you wash your hands and rub them together really fast.
- Water bubbles and boils at 212 degrees Fahrenheit.
- Pop Rocks bubble when you pour them in your mouth.
- Lava bubbles and flows from volcanoes at more than 2,140 degrees.

Lots of things bubble, including anger. Rarely does a person go from being totally calm to super angry in an instant. Many times anger starts as frustration or disappointment. When frustration grows, it can bubble over into an angry outburst.

Try to picture anger like a volcano. Before a volcano erupts, it shakes, quakes, and gives off gas. This same thing happens when you get angry. (Okay, maybe without the gas.) It can be a slow process as your feelings bubble inside you like molten lava. Unless you can let off some steam, you're going to explode. That's why some people call getting angry "blowing your top."

Everybody gets angry. Even Jesus got mad (check out John 2:13–16). When most of us lose our temper, we do things we regret and don't represent God well with our actions. We may hit somebody (or something), kick the couch, or call somebody a name.

In the Psalms, King David encouraged us to refrain from anger and give up our *rage* (Psalm 37:8). Rage means uncontrollable anger. It's a good word to remember, because rage always leads to something bad.

Later in the Bible, the apostle Paul told us to not sin by letting anger control us (Ephesians 4:26). Instead of being out of control, we need to control our feelings of anger and not let them turn to rage. That may sound impossible. But Jesus did it, and He can help us do it too.

Refrain from anger and give up your rage; do not be agitated—it can only bring harm.
—Psalm 37:8

DEFEND YOUR FAITH

The next time you start to feel angry, take some time to think about what's causing your frustration. Count to ten to calm down. Try to picture the frustration bubbles inside of you going away. Think about what you're going to say and do next. Then pray to God to give you self-control.

Anger doesn't have to turn you into a raging pool of lava. By learning to control your anger, you will be able to avoid doing something destructive when you're upset. Remember that Jesus came to show you a better way to live. Even when Jesus got angry, He was able to honor God with His actions and not sin. That's not easy, but with God's help you can do it.

A Ring of Truth

In 2018, archaeologists announced the discovery of a two-thousand-year-old ring that gives validity to one of the most important stories in the New Testament. This ring was actually found in Jerusalem in the late 1960s. However, nobody thought it was anything special. With modern technology, scientists discovered the ring had an inscription on it. The words "of Pilatus" were carved into the metal. If that name rings a bell, it should. Pontius Pilate was the Roman governor who conducted Jesus' trial and ultimately condemned Him to death.

According to dates in the Bible, Pilate ruled from AD 26–36. But for hundreds of years, some people didn't believe Pilate was a real person because archaeologists hadn't dug up any evidence that proved his existence. That changed in 1961, when researchers found a stone that featured the carved words, "Pontius Pilate, Prefect of Judea." (Read more about the "Pilate Stone" in the *Defend Your Faith Bible*.) The inscription on the ring discovered in 2018 provides further evidence that the Bible's story of Jesus' death and resurrection is true.

The ring is made of copper, a not-so-valuable metal. Copper was not something a high-ranking official would typically wear. This has led archaeologists to believe the ring belonged to one of Pontius Pilate's servants. With the ring—called a signet ring—a servant could act for a ruler or seal a letter with the ruler's mark to give the document authority and power.

"To all who did receive him, he gave them the right to be children of God, to those who believe in his name."—John 1:12

DEFEND YOUR FAITH

Using a leader's seal or name made a document legally binding. This was done by placing a dab of wax on an order and then pressing a signet ring into the wax to leave the leader's mark.

In Bible times, being able to use the king's seal was a high honor. You can find references to a signet ring in the story of Esther and Mordecai (see Esther 3:10 and 8:2). Evil Queen Jezebel used King Ahab's signet ring to set up a murder plot (see 1 Kings 21:8). King Darius sealed Daniel in the lions' den by using his signet ring and the rings of his nobles (see Daniel 6:17).

Signet rings aren't talked about much in the New Testament. But through believing in the name of Jesus Christ, you have a sort of spiritual signet ring. Jesus, the King of kings, stamps you with His seal of approval when you put your faith in Him. You become His child, gaining the right to ask things of God in His name. Jesus said you'll be able to do amazing works for Him (John 14:12). What's more, when you pray in Jesus' name, it's like marking your request with His authority and power.

WASH AWAY WORRY

Right now about 1,800 thunderstorms are booming somewhere around the world. Scientists estimate lightning strikes the earth one hundred times every second.

As powerful as storms can be, God is even more powerful. The righteous man Job pointed out that God established a limit for rain and a path for lightning. Although Job was talking about God's power and wisdom, his description also sounds a lot like the water cycle. In God's wisdom, He created water to be renewable. The water cycle is the path through which water moves around the Earth. Sun heats the water, creating evaporation and transporting water vapor into the air. The water vapor turns into clouds as it cools. The clouds float over the land and rain down water. Then the cycle starts again.

Isn't it cool how God is the first and ultimate recycler? The water cycle is amazing, and it also causes some amazing storms. Fortunately, the National Weather Service estimates that your chances of being hit by lightning are about one in 1.2 million. That means you have a much better chance of becoming a supermodel or playing professional basketball.

Even if we know the facts, many of us may worry about being struck by lightning (or about lots of other things that will probably never happen). Worry is natural. We can't help but worry about our future. But watch out when worry crosses over into fear. God doesn't want us to be afraid, because it wastes our time and shows that we don't fully trust Him.

When God fixed the weight of the wind and distributed the water by measure, when he established a limit for the rain and a path for the lightning, he considered wisdom and evaluated it.—Job 28:25–27

DEFEND YOUR FAITH

Get a piece of paper and write "Pros" on one side and "Cons" on the other. Now list all of the positive and negative things about worrying. The positives of worrying include . . . well, nothing. Worrying never helps your situation. The negatives of worry are numerous, including being tired, irritable, stressed, and depressed.

The Bible says, "Can any of you add one moment to his life span by worrying?" (Matthew 6:27). The answer is a thundering no! Instead of worrying, pray and give your fears over to God. You can always rest easy knowing that a powerfully wise God is in control. God doesn't want you to dwell on fear and bad thoughts. He wants you to be wise—letting your worries wash away by thinking about His goodness and all the blessings He provides. After all, fresh water through the water cycle is only a tiny splash of God's ocean of blessings.

IDOL THOUGHTS

Do you have any silly superstitions?

When some kids find a penny on the ground, they pick it up . . . so all day they'll have good luck. Other students have a lucky shirt they wear during big tests. If you look around, you might discover people follow lots of different superstitions.

• Some people think a rabbit's foot brings good luck, so they put one on a keychain and carry it around.

• Baseball teams will often put on their "rally caps" late in games by flipping their hats inside out and wearing them backwards on their heads. They believe it'll help their team score runs.

• Tennis great Serena Williams wears the same pair of socks during a tournament. Since she's won over $92 million playing tennis, she could definitely afford another pair.

Do you think following superstitions actually helps? Would Serena have won hundreds of tennis tournaments if she changed her socks? Probably. Would a student score just as high on a test if his "lucky" shirt was in the laundry? Most likely.

Although superstitions aren't necessarily evil, they become harmful when they cause us to put our trust in "things" instead of in God.

The first two Ten Commandments (the most important rules in the Old Testament) say basically the same thing: do not worship anything besides God.

Although God clearly spelled it out, God's people didn't follow His command. Over and over again, they turned from God and worshipped idols. An *idol* is a physical creation that is worshipped. After God freed the Israelites from slavery in Egypt and restored their nation, the people worshipped a golden calf and statues of false gods. The results were devastating. Their nation crumbled, and many people were taken into captivity. The prophet Jeremiah explained why disaster came to the Israelites. And it boiled down to two words: idol worship.

Because you burned incense and sinned against the LORD and didn't obey the LORD and didn't follow his instruction, his statutes, and his testimonies, this disaster has come to you.—Jeremiah 44:23

DEFEND YOUR FAITH

Idols may seem like a thing of the past, but anything that fills your thoughts above God is an idol. Some people put their trust in money. Others spend their time seeking popularity or trying to be the best at a video game.

Identify the potential idols in your life by thinking about the activities that consume the most time. Do you have any superstitions that you follow above God? Knowing God's laws and following His instructions are important. And always remember that it's God who supplies all your needs and gives you success—not some silly superstition or idol.

IT'S A MIRACLE

Thirty years ago, it would've been hard to imagine a person soaring above the earth on a platform of tiny drones. (Warning: Don't try this at home!) And nobody could have guessed that doctors would be able to perform surgery on a patient thousands of miles away using TV cameras and robotic arms. That's amazing.

Speaking of TVs, companies have developed screens so thin that they come rolled up in a tube. Simply unroll the screen, mount it on a wall, and voilà—instant theater.

When you look at technological advances, it's easy to think we live in an age of miracles. But the true age of miracles occurred thousands of years ago when Jesus came to earth.

The books of Matthew, Mark, Luke, and John record more than thirty of Jesus' miracles. He healed the sick, caused the lame to walk, opened the eyes of the blind, raised the dead to life, fed more than five thousand people with one lunch, cast out evil spirits, caused a coin to appear in the mouth of a fish, walked on water, and much more!

Looking at a list is pretty amazing. But consider this fact: Jesus did lots of other miracles that aren't even recorded in the Bible.

Read through the Gospels or go to a website with your parents that lists Jesus' miracles. Some Bibles even have a list in the back. Which miracle amazes you the most?

Do you know why Jesus performed miracles? Some of His miracles fulfilled prophecies that were written down hundreds of years before He was born. But the apostle John provided an answer to that question in John 20:31 when he wrote, "These are written so that you may believe that Jesus is the Messiah, the Son of God, and that by believing you may have life in his name."

Jesus performed many other signs in the presence of his disciples that are not written in this book.—John 20:30

DEFEND YOUR FAITH

Jesus wanted to show the world that He was the promised Messiah. He came to save and heal. Not only did He perform the ultimate miracle by dying and rising from the dead to save us from our sins, but He physically healed people as a sign of His power. Nothing could keep Jesus from doing everything the Father sent Him to do.

We may not be able to witness Jesus heal a leper or feed thousands of hungry people with a single granola bar today. But when you stop and look around, you can see God at work. The same God who performed miracles thousands of years ago, still performs them today.

JESUS WAS NO IMPOSTER

Frank Abagnale was an imposter. As a teenager he pretended to be a commercial airline pilot, a doctor, and a lawyer. He was so convincing that people were fooled. Frank flew more than one million miles for free and made a lot of money as a con man. But Frank got caught. After serving years in prison, he worked with the FBI for over forty years to catch other fakers.

At the beginning of Jesus' ministry, many religious leaders believed He was an imposter. They'd heard of His miracles and wise teachings but wondered how Jesus could know so much when He hadn't studied under a famous rabbi. These religious leaders knew the prophecies of a coming Messiah. Jesus didn't fit the picture they imagined. *He must be a fake!* they thought. *And we have to catch him.*

The Pharisees saw their chance to catch Jesus when He was speaking to a large crowd. In the middle of His teaching, a paralyzed man was lowered through the roof to be healed. Seeing the faith of the man and his friends, Jesus told the man his sins were forgiven. The religious leaders immediately thought, *Who can forgive sins but God alone?*

Jesus knew the leaders' thoughts. Only God had the authority to forgive, and they didn't believe Jesus was God. With the paralyzed man lying at His feet, Jesus looked at the religious leaders and asked a question about whether it was easier to forgive sin or heal the lame. After asking the question, Jesus called Himself the Son of Man, which was how the prophet Daniel referred to the coming Messiah.

"Which is easier: to say, 'Your sins are forgiven,' or to say, 'Get up and walk'?"
—Luke 5:23

DEFEND YOUR FAITH

Was Jesus' question some kind of trick? No. Jesus wanted the religious leaders to come up with the answer: forgiving and healing are equally easy for God to do, and they're both impossibly hard for a human to do.

The Pharisees must have thought Jesus was bluffing. Surely Jesus wouldn't tell the man "get up and walk," because the moment the man wasn't healed, everyone would know Jesus was a fraud.

Jesus knew their thoughts as well. He told the paralyzed man to get up and go home—and the man did. His stood up, grabbed his mat, and walked!

With that one miracle, Jesus proved He had God's power and authority to heal, which also proved He had God's authority to forgive sin. Jesus didn't just forgive and heal a paralyzed man that day. He also did something that we never want to forget. He proved that He was God—and not an imposter.

WHAT CAN MY PET TEACH ME ABOUT GOD?

Do you have a pet? Fish are the most popular pet in the world. They're just really hard to cuddle with.

Cats and dogs are the second and third most common pet—in that order. Researchers have found that dog owners tend to be more social and accepting people, and cat owners are more introverted and creative.

Whether you own a dog, cat, bird, or salamander, you probably love them very much. But what if they make a mess in your room? Do you love them any less? How about if they climb on your bed and wake you up in the middle of the night or run away from time to time? Then there are those other "messes" pets create. Does cleaning up after them change how much you love them? If you answered no to those questions, then you have something called *unconditional love* for your pet.

To love unconditionally means there's no situation that could make you stop loving. You love not because of anything your pets do for you, but because you have *chosen* to love them. You love your pets even if they make a mess, because they mean more to you than any trouble they may cause.

And that's exactly how God loves us as His children. Did you know that there's nothing you could possibly do to make God love you any more or any less than He does right now? The apostle Paul listed ten examples of things in Romans that won't separate a believer from God's love.

"I am persuaded that neither . . . things present nor things to come . . . nor any other created thing will be able to separate us from the love of God that is in Christ Jesus our Lord."—Romans 8:38–39

DEFEND YOUR FAITH

When you read through the entire list in your Bible, you'll notice it covers every possible situation that could happen. In other words, there is nothing in life or in the universe that will ever change God's unconditional love for you. Nothing that has been created can stop Him from loving you. And since you are a creation of God, even *you* can't do anything that would change His love for you!

The words *unconditional love* never appear in the Bible, but God's Word does say His love is *eternal*, *perfect*, *everlasting*, *abounding*, and *forever*.

The next time you cuddle up with your dog or cat—or bird or salamander—and feel that warm, fuzzy feeling, think about this: you're getting just a small taste of how much your heavenly Father loves you. You can run away from God and make a mess of things, but God loves you the same. Parents sometimes say pets teach responsibility. That's true. Now you know they give you a glimpse of God's unconditional love too.

LISTENING TO THE WRONG VOICES

It's wise to be a good listener. But we also have to choose the right voices to listen to. Listening to your mom or dad? Smart. Listening to friends who are caught up in popular culture and popular opinions? Not so smart.

The first four books of the New Testament include an interaction between Jesus and a Roman governor named Pontius Pilate. After the envious religious leaders had Jesus arrested, they brought Him before Pilate. Their plan? Convince the governor to have Jesus executed.

Pilate questioned Jesus but couldn't find anything Jesus had done that deserved punishment. Pilate knew Jesus was innocent and that the religious leaders wanted Him killed because of their own jealousy. Pilate's wife even sent him an urgent message, telling Pilate to "have nothing to do with that righteous man" (Matthew 27:19). She had seen the truth about Jesus in a dream and didn't want her husband to condemn Him.

At the end of the day, three "voices" were speaking to Pilate:

- The voice inside his head saying Jesus was innocent and should be set free.
- The voice of Pilate's wife who felt the same.
- The voices of the religious leaders and the crowd demanding Jesus be crucified.

Who did Pilate listen to? Sadly, he listened to the wrong voices—and made a really bad decision as a result. But why would Pilate ignore the voice inside him and his wife's voice too? Mark 15:15 gives us the answer. He wanted to satisfy the crowd.

"But they kept up the pressure, demanding with loud voices that he be crucified, and their voices won out. So Pilate decided to grant their demand."—Luke 23:23–24

DEFEND YOUR FAITH

It's easy for us to criticize Pilate for his decision. But sometimes we do the same thing. Mom or Dad, other family members, and even our conscience tell us to do one thing, but friends urge us to do something different. Going against the crowd is difficult. We can be like Pilate, wanting to satisfy friends or people around us—instead of doing what God says is right.

Do you think Pilate ever regretted giving in to the wrong voices? Probably so. Even though it was all part of God's plan for Jesus to be crucified, Pilate had to live with the consequences of his decision.

Following God isn't always easy. The Bible and your parents can give you good advice. But you may feel a lot of pressure from your friends to go a different direction. Be careful to listen to—and obey—the right voices so you don't have regrets too.

DEFAMER FACTS
NAME: *PONTIUS PILATE*
PLACE: *JERUSALEM*
TIME: *ABOUT AD 30*

A HELPING HAND ... OR BEAK

Some birds are just lazy.

Have you ever seen a photo of a grayish bird with a bright yellow eyespot and orange beak riding on the back of a zebra? Maybe you've seen this same bird sitting on the back of a gazelle, water buffalo, or rhinoceros. When it comes to getting around the African plain, oxpeckers aren't picky. They'll ride on almost anything.

The interesting thing is that the animal Ubers don't seem to mind having a tiny hitchhiker on their backs. That's because oxpeckers eat all the ticks, pests, and blood-sucking bugs off their ride's body. It may sound gross, but it's a win-win situation. The oxpecker gets a free trip and ready-made food source. The zebra gets rid of nasty insects that could hurt it.

This is just one example of a mutually beneficial relationship between animals. God created many situations where animals help each other.

Take the sea anemone. Most fish look at an anemone as their enemy because its wavy tentacles pack a powerful sting. But the colorful clownfish can swim unharmed through a sea anemone.

In this case, the clownfish benefits because the anemone protects it from predators. The anemone also wins, because when other fish follow the clownfish too closely, they swim into the anemone's tentacles and become its next meal.

"Ask the animals, and they will instruct you; ask the birds of the sky, and they will tell you. . . . Let the fish of the sea inform you. Which of all these does not know that the hand of the LORD has done this? The life of every living thing is in his hand."—Job 12:7–10

DEFEND YOUR FAITH

Isn't it cool how God created animals to help each other? God's character shows up in so much of creation. From the orderliness of human DNA to the intricate design of flowers, His creativity is everywhere.

We can learn a lot by studying animals. When we look at birds that care for bigger beasts, it reminds us to have compassionate hearts and helpful spirits to reach out to people in need—even if they're bigger than us. As we see how God provides food and homes for all creatures, it demonstrates how He holds every living thing in His hand.

We serve a caring God, and we should care for people too. The next time you see an opportunity to help someone . . . do it. Maybe you'll have to give up some sleep to visit an assisted living home on a Saturday morning or share your lunch with someone who doesn't have enough to eat. Not only will you feel good because you helped, but the one in need will feel better too—just like the oxpecker and zebra.

THE TRUE KING OF KINGS

The modern-day country of Iraq covers the lands of several Old Testament hot spots such as Assyria and Babylon. You know about Adam and Eve. Biblical experts believe the Garden of Eden could have been located in Iraq. Noah? He probably built the ark in Iraq. Abraham? Born in Iraq. Even the fishy prophet Jonah preached to people in Nineveh, which is where? You guessed it—Iraq!

So when archaeologists dig around in Iraq, they find all kinds of items related to the Old Testament. In 2018 archaeologists were sifting through rubble and tunnels in ancient Nineveh when they came upon some wall inscriptions. One inscription told about a troop of monkeys and perhaps the first lion in a zoo! But a more significant writing mentioned a king named Esar-haddon.

King Esar-haddon is mentioned several times in the Old Testament: Isaiah 37:37–38, Ezra 4:2, and 2 Kings 19:37. This mighty conqueror ruled Assyria for twelve years (681–669 BC). One of the 2,700-year-old wall inscriptions said, "The palace of Esarhaddon, strong king, king of the world, king of Assyria, governor of Babylon, king of Sumer and Akkad, king of the kings of lower Egypt, upper Egypt and Kush."

Although King Esar-haddon wasn't really the king of the world, this mention of him contributes to the credibility of the Bible. If the Bible writers got the historic details correct, like a specific king, we can trust their stories about God and His people are true.

"The Lamb will conquer them because he is Lord of lords and King of kings. Those with him are called, chosen, and faithful."
—Revelation 17:14

DEFEND YOUR FAITH

Did you notice the phrase "king of kings" in the inscription? In Bible times, that description was a way of showing great honor. Archaeologists have found it on ancient plaques, clay tablets, stones, and walls. The Old Testament uses the phrase to describe Artaxerxes (Ezra 7:12) and Nebuchadnezzar (Ezekiel 26:7).

Seven hundred years later, New Testament writers used those words too. Both the apostles Paul and John called Jesus the "King of kings" (1 Timothy 6:15; Revelation 17:14, 19:16).

Did you notice when Jesus is called "King of kings" that the first *K* is capitalized? That means Jesus is the Boss, the Head Honcho, the best and truest King who ever lived or ever will live. He is the ruler of all kings, living, dead, or in the future. The last book of the Bible shows how Jesus wins—He conquers all. Knowing that Jesus is the King of kings gives us a sense of peace in uncertain times. We know how the story ends. Jesus is victorious, and we're with Him as His called and faithful people.

BRINGER OF PEACE

The Colosseum in ancient Rome was a brutal place. Gladiators fought to the death. Criminals were torn apart by ferocious animals. People suffered unthinkable tortures. And it was all for entertainment. (That makes reality TV seem pretty tame, huh?)

Then in around AD 404, a Christian named Telemachus traveled from Asia to Rome. He followed the crowds into the Colosseum and was horrified by what he saw—people killing and torturing each other for the crowd's amusement.

Telemachus stood up and shouted, "In the name of Christ, forbear!" (which means, "Stop what you're doing, because God doesn't like it!"). But the crowd's cheers drowned out his pleas.

The small man walked down the aisle and made his way to the floor of the Colosseum to get the crowd's attention. Again, Telemachus shouted, "In the name of Christ, forbear!"

Noticing the strange visitor, the gladiators stopped fighting. Suddenly, all eyes were on Telemachus. But instead of turning from their barbaric ways, the crowd grew angry. They wanted the show to go on. They threw food, stones, and other heavy objects at Telemachus. And they didn't stop throwing things until Telemachus was dead.

When the emperor of Rome learned what happened to this humble man, the gladiator games stopped for good.

During nearly four hundred years of competition, more than 400,000 people died in the Colosseum. By speaking up, Telemachus ended the killing once and for all.

"Blessed are the peacemakers, for they will be called sons of God."—Matthew 5:9

Defend Your Faith

What do you think of this true story? Is it sad or happy? Maybe it's both. By standing up for peace and God's truth, Telemachus changed history. This one man impacted an entire kingdom. He used his life to save other lives.

You can use your words to help others too. God wants you to keep your cool and speak out for His truth. In the book of Proverbs, King Solomon wrote, "A hot-tempered person stirs up conflict, but one slow to anger calms strife" (5:18).

When you find yourself in a situation where an injustice is happening, pray, and ask God for wisdom. If you see bullies picking on someone, maybe you could crack a joke to lighten the mood or speak up and say, "Stop." You may also need to calmly get an adult to handle the problem.

Don't ignore abuse or injustice; and don't put yourself in any danger. But do be a peacemaker and make a difference for God.

Defender Facts
Name: *Telemachus*
Place: *Rome*
Time: *Around AD 400*

ANGELS AMONG US

The word *angel* appears nearly three hundred times in the Bible. That's a lot. But we know the names of only a few angels. The angel Gabriel famously appeared to Mary and told her she'd give birth to God's Son. Michael is called the archangel (Jude 9) and is a powerful warrior. Those are good angels.

We also know the names of two bad angels—Satan and Abaddon. Satan, also known as the Devil, was an angel that tried to overthrow God and was cast out of heaven. Abaddon seems to be Satan's archangel (Revelation 9:11).

How much do you really know about angels? Answer these questions to find out.

1. Angels have wings.   True/False
2. Angels are scary.   True/False
3. Humans turn into angels when we die. True/False
4. Angels have different jobs.   True/False
5. Each person has a guardian angel.   True/False

Answers:

1. True (sometimes). The Bible doesn't say all angels have wings, but some do (Exodus 25:20, Isaiah 6:2).

2. True. Nearly every time an angel shows up, it says, "Do not be afraid" (Luke 1:13, 1:30, and 2:10). If they aren't scary, angels are certainly startling.

3. False. Humans and angels are separate beings created differently by God. When people who know Jesus die, they receive heavenly bodies (1 Corinthians 15:51–54).

4. True. The word *angel* means "messenger." The Bible describes angels as worshipping God, delivering messages, protecting humans, battling evil, and giving comfort.

5. False. The Bible says angels help people, but it doesn't say each person has an angel watching over them like a bodyguard.

*He will give his angels orders concerning you,
to protect you in all your ways.—Psalm 91:11*

DEFEND YOUR FAITH

How did you do in the quiz? If you got three or four correct, that's good. Many people have messed-up ideas about angels because TV commercials or cartoons show them sitting on clouds and playing harps. But angels don't sit around. They're busy. They're powerful. And they're ready to do God's bidding.

God has specific jobs for angels. One of those is protecting His people. God's angels guard you in ways that you'll never know or comprehend. As humans we're not always aware when an angel is around us. Hebrews 13:2 says people have entertained angels without knowing it. Even if we never see an angel, we can be confident they're around—and doing God's work.

Take a few minutes to make a detailed list in your mind of what you know about angels. You might think: *powerful*, *never die*, *watch over me*. Then pray and thank God for His angels.

A QUESTION FROM THE CROSS

While Jesus hung on the cross, He made six statements and asked one question. Take a look, because these words tell us a lot about God's Son.

Statement 1: "Father, forgive them, because they do not know what they are doing" (Luke 23:34). Jesus looked down on the soldiers who had driven nails into His hands and feet, and He asked for God to forgive them.

Statement 2: "Truly I tell you, today you will be with me in paradise" (Luke 23:43). Jesus was crucified between two criminals. One recognized that Jesus was the innocent Messiah. He asked to come into God's kingdom, and Jesus promised he would.

Statement 3: "Woman, here is your son. . . . Here is your mother" (John 19:26–27). Jesus saw Mary and His disciple John, and He told them to take care of each other.

Statement 4: "I'm thirsty" (John 19:28). Crucifixion was a brutal way to die. Jesus suffered physically and asked for a drink.

Statement 5: "It is finished" (John 19:30). Jesus knew the work He'd come to do on earth was over. His death would pay the penalty for the sins of the world.

Statement 6: "Father, into your hands I entrust my spirit" (Luke 23:46). Jesus spoke those words and died. In His last breath, Jesus showed His faith in His heavenly Father.

In the middle of these amazing statements, Jesus also asked a question: "My God, my God, why have you abandoned me?" (Matthew 27:46).

"He himself has said, 'I will never leave you or abandon you. . . . The Lord is my helper; I will not be afraid.'"—Hebrews 13:5–6

DEFEND YOUR FAITH

Jesus' question is actually a quote from the first verse of Psalm 22. Jesus knew the Scriptures, and He knew that later in this psalm it reaffirms that God is holy and can be trusted. Jesus trusted His heavenly Father to the end, even when He felt abandoned.

The Greek word Jesus used for "abandoned" is a very scary word. It means to leave someone behind in a helpless and dangerous situation. At that moment, Jesus was separated for the first time from His Father and Holy Spirit as He took the punishment for our sins. Sin separates us from God. Jesus paid for all sin on the cross. He was separated from His Father so that you never will be.

In Hebrews 13:5, that same Greek word is used when God says He will never leave us or *abandon* us. As a believer in Jesus, you have been forgiven because He fully paid for your sins. When Jesus said, "It is finished," it was like He was saying, "Paid in full!" Jesus paid the full price for your sin. And there is no question about that!

WHY IS WISDOM SO VALUABLE?

Where on earth do miners find raw silver?

Ha! It's a trick question. Raw silver isn't found *on* earth; it's found *under* the ground. You have to dig to discover this precious metal. To search for silver, you need the right tools. Would you take a toothbrush? A comb? Crayons? No, you would use a shovel, gloves, and a pickax.

King Solomon said if we search for wisdom with the same effort we would use to search for silver or hidden treasure, then we will discover the knowledge of God (Proverbs 2:4–5). That knowledge is the beginning of wisdom, because wisdom comes from God.

Just like silver isn't lying on the ground, wisdom isn't easy to see at first either. We have to dig with the right tools. In this case, the right tool is the Bible. As you read God's Word and follow the things you learn, you will find the hidden treasure of God's wisdom.

The Bible says this wisdom is even more valuable than silver and gold. But how can that be?

Many people confuse wisdom with knowledge. *Knowledge* is basically accumulating facts. You go to school to gain knowledge. *Wisdom* is the ability to apply that knowledge into making good decisions. Knowing that gravity is the force that pulls down on objects shows you have smarts. Not jumping off a cliff shows you are wise.

When you read the Bible, you learn that God is kind, loving, just, giving, and powerful. He should be respected and put first in your life. His ways are above anything we could understand. That's the beginning of wisdom.

"Happy is a man who finds wisdom and who acquires understanding, for she is more profitable than silver, and her revenue is better than gold. She is more precious than jewels; nothing you desire can equal her."
—Proverbs 3:13–15

DEFEND YOUR FAITH

So how do you put knowledge into action? By praising God, helping others, and asking for His direction. Acting with godly wisdom may not make you popular or rich. But it will bring you joy, peace, love for others, and many other things that silver and treasure can't buy. God created you to find joy by knowing Him as your Savior and best Friend. Nobody is truly fulfilled without understanding who they are in God. Money, possessions, and power can't bring happiness. King Solomon wrote about that in the book after Proverbs, called Ecclesiastes. Godly wisdom helps you make hard decisions and feel satisfied in all situations. Joy, peace, and contentment are priceless. That's what God's wisdom provides, and that's why it's so valuable.

WHEN GOD SEEMS HARSH

King David wanted to bring the ark of the covenant—the symbol of God's presence—to Jerusalem. He organized a huge parade for the event. David gathered thirty-thousand men and all kinds of musicians for the celebration.

The ark was put on a cart pulled by oxen and wheeled toward Jerusalem. When the oxen stumbled, a man named Uzzah reached out to keep the ark from falling . . . and God struck him dead (see 2 Samuel 6:7).

Why would God do that? you might think.

Well, in Numbers 7:6–9, God made it very clear that the holy things, such as the ark of the covenant, were not to be hauled in a cart like luggage. The ark of the covenant had to be *carried* by priests to show reverence for God. In Numbers 4:15, God made it clear that anyone who touched the holy things, other than the priests, would die. If the ark had been carried by priests—like God told them to do— Uzzah would never have needed to put a hand on it. And since God said anyone touching the ark would die, He had to keep His word.

King David wanted to do a good thing by bringing the ark to Jerusalem. But he hadn't been careful to do it the right way. He didn't obey the clear guidelines in God's Word.

Did the ark of the covenant ever make it to Jerusalem? Yes, three months later. This time David was careful to follow exactly what God's Word said. Priests carried the ark, and everyone enjoyed the parade.

DEFEND YOUR FAITH

You might read the story of Uzzah and think, *God was too harsh*.

That's the view many people have of God. They think God has too many rules and dishes out too many harsh punishments. But that's why it's important to know God's Word. When David looked back at the Scriptures, he discovered what was right and wrong. Disobeying God has consequences. But God doesn't kill or punish people randomly. He's a reasonable and rational God who makes the rules.

Through the story of moving the ark of the covenant, God made a simple truth really clear to King David, His people, and us today. Doing a right thing in the wrong way is still wrong. We need to respect God enough to do things the way He tells us. His instructions are meant for our own good. His rules protect us.

If we don't obey, we really can't blame God when things don't turn out like we'd hoped. In the end, God isn't harsh . . . He's holy.

HAVE YOU HERD?

Scientists have found animals often conform to *herd behavior*. Sheep flock together and follow a leader to find food, water, or rest. Small rodents called lemmings go where the head of the pack goes. Even earthworms travel underground in herds, doing what the leader does.

Many times living in a herd benefits animals. Researchers have found cattle that live in herds are actually smarter because they learn from the leader. Being part of a herd also keeps animals safe. They watch out for each other and look bigger to predators. A herd of zebras can be especially confusing to a cheetah, because the combination of black and white stripes makes it difficult for the big cat to distinguish one zebra from the next.

Herds are helpful, but they can hurt too. Sometimes sheep follow their herd into the slaughterhouse. Lemmings are famous for following their pack by jumping off a cliff into the water in hopes of swimming to a new home. For good— and sometimes for bad—animals tend to go along with what the rest of the herd is doing.

Following blindly in a group may sound silly, but scientists say humans can fall into the same pattern. It's called a *herd mentality*. We fit our behavior into what the people around us are doing, even if it means ignoring our own feelings and beliefs.

Sometimes following our friends is okay; however, many times our parents and God expect more. Unlike animals that instinctively follow the herd without thinking, God gave us a brain to make good decisions. The "group" shouldn't be our guide, because God gave us better ones: the Bible and the Holy Spirit.

Do not be conformed to this age, but be
transformed by the renewing of your mind,
so that you may discern what is the good,
pleasing, and perfect will of God.
—Romans 12:2

DEFEND YOUR FAITH

Conforming to the patterns of this world, just like following the crowd, is easy. Unfortunately, if we go with the crowd too often in our choice of music, fashion, and movies, we'll find ourselves far from God's path for our lives.

God wants us to be different. Humans didn't evolve from animals. We were created unique. Instead of conforming, we can use the amazing brain God gave us and act like the amazing image-bearers of God that we are. And we do that by renewing our minds through reading His Word and growing closer to Him.

When you dare to be different for God, it may take you in a different direction from most people. You may get teased. It's "safer" to blend into the herd and be a follower. But God created you to stand out, not blend in. You were made for adventure and to glorify Him.

So don't be a lemming. Be a leader . . . and follow God's will for your life.

THE DIFFERENCE BETWEEN HAPPINESS AND JOY

After the Super Bowl, players from both professional football teams share some similarities:

- They are physically and emotionally exhausted.
- They are battered and bruised from playing the brutal game of football.

But there are tremendous differences between the teams as well.

- The players from the losing team look tired, discouraged, and unhappy—like they're feeling the pain.
- Players on the winning team jump around and celebrate the victory, even though they're as worn-out as the losers. Being on the winning team helps these players experience a joy that goes deeper than their physical circumstances.

In a small way, this scene illustrates the difference between happiness and joy. We're happy when everything goes our way, when we get what we want, when we're feeling good, or when we hear great news. Happiness depends on everything around us going just right.

Joy goes deeper. *Joy* is a state of delight that comes from knowing God. Joy can't be gained through our own efforts. It's a fruit of the Spirit (see Galatians 5:22–23) that grows within us. Just like the players on the winning Super Bowl team, followers of Jesus can always have a deep sense of victory because Christ defeated death! He forgives freely and prepares a place for us in heaven.

Even if everything goes wrong—our plans don't work out, or we get really bad news—we can still have joy.

Do not grieve, because the joy of the LORD is your strength.—Nehemiah 8:10

DEFEND YOUR FAITH

When bad things happen, it's easy to be unhappy. Happiness is a feeling that comes and goes. Joy lasts, because it comes from our faith in God and from understanding all He does for us. Because of joy, we can feel excited about the future, even when we're tired and discouraged. The choice is ours. Remember:

- Jesus promises to never leave us (Hebrews 13:5–6).
- God's love is unfailing (Psalm 32:10).
- God has a purpose for us (Ephesians 2:10).
- God promises to work out even the hard things for our good (Romans 8:28).

Remembering these truths brings joy. And through that joy, we gain God's strength to make it through the hardest times.

So if you feel like happiness is hard to find, realize you're looking for the wrong thing. Look at everything God does (and has done), and you'll find something better than happiness: real joy.

THE KIND LEADING THE BLIND

The Bible is full of amazing military victories. Gideon and 300 men defeated an army of more than 100,000. Jonathan and his armor-bearer beat a stronghold of Philistine soldiers. Samson toppled an entire evil temple in God's strength. But one of the most impressive victories in the Old Testament occurred during a battle that was never fought.

In 2 Kings 6:8–23, we read about a massive army with horses and chariots being sent to capture *one* man: Elisha. This great man of God had protected Israel from the king of Aram. Every time Aram came up with a plan to destroy Israel, God told Elisha exactly what the enemy was plotting. The enemy king became furious. He realized he'd never beat Israel unless he captured Elisha first.

When the Aramean army surrounded the city where Elisha was staying, his servant was terrified. But Elisha wasn't one bit afraid. He saw something that his servant couldn't.

"Lord," Elisha prayed, "please open his eyes and let him see."

Suddenly, the servant saw a huge army—God's army—there to protect them.

"Blind the enemy," Elisha prayed.

Instantly, every Aramean soldier stumbled around, unable to see. Elisha walked up to his enemies. "Follow me," he said. "I'll take you to the man you're looking for."

Like a parade, Elisha led the blind army to Samaria, where Israel's king and army lived. Elisha prayed that the enemy soldiers would see again. Their blindness disappeared. To their shock, they saw they were surrounded and trapped!

The king of Israel saw a chance to defeat the enemy army. He asked Elisha, "Should I kill them?"

"No," Elisha said. "Give them food and water, and let them go back to their master."

Now it was the king of Israel's turn to be shocked. But he obeyed. He prepared a great feast for the enemy, and then he set them free.

"If your enemy is hungry, feed him. If he is thirsty, give him something to drink. . . . Do not be conquered by evil, but conquer evil with good."—Romans 12:20–21

DEFEND YOUR FAITH

The Aramean soldiers were amazed at Elisha's kindness and God's power. After returning home and telling the king or Aram what happened, the Arameans stopped being so mean to Israel.

Elisha didn't win this battle with his own might. He had the power of God behind him. Plus, he conquered with kindness.

When people are really mean to you, remember this story. Think of your "enemy" as blind and needing someone to guide them. Through your example, you can show them how to live differently. Don't return evil for evil. Be kind, and see how God can change hearts.

DEFENDER FACTS
NAME: *ELISHA*
PLACE: *ISRAEL*
TIME: *ABOUT 840 BC*

A TEST YOU WANT TO PASS

Do you know why teachers give you tests? Is it because they're mean?

No. Although tests aren't much fun, they're meant for your benefit. You get tested in school so your teacher knows what you learned and can see areas where you need improvement. A good grade shows that you're learning the subject. But if you miss a lot of questions, it reveals a need to increase your understanding and to study more.

The Bible has a lot to say about tests. Many times Scripture uses the word *trials* to refer to tests. These trials pop up in our lives as relationship struggles, disappointments, or other problems. God doesn't allow these trials because He's mean. He allows trials so we grow closer to Him and become more like Jesus. Jesus said we will all have suffering in this life, so we need to be courageous (John 16:33).

Because trials are a fact of life, we shouldn't be afraid of them. Instead of fearing tests, God's tells us to rejoice when we're tested.

Wouldn't it be great if you never had to take another test? That might sound good at first. Some kids fake a sickness to try and avoid tests at school. Other people ask God to take away all their problems in life so they're never tested. But without tests, we'll never change, grow, and push ourselves to be more like Jesus.

You rejoice in this, even though now for a short time, if necessary, you suffer grief in various trials so that the proven character of your faith—more valuable than gold which, though perishable, is refined by fire—may result in praise, glory, and honor at the revelation of Jesus Christ.—1 Peter 1:6–7

DEFEND YOUR FAITH

Which do you think is a better prayer in the middle of a test?

a. "God, please take away this test so everything is perfect in my life."

b. "God, please give me the strength to make it through this test and become more like You."

When you go through difficult times, don't give up. Rely on God's strength, and watch your faith grow. As you persevere through life's trials, you learn from your mistakes and change for the better.

You won't always get an A on a test—in school or in life. But if you want to be more like Jesus, you'll rejoice when tests come because it means God is showing you where you need to change. And with God's help, you can pass the test.

FRUIT FOR THOUGHT

Tomatoes are the most popular fruit in the world. (Yes, tomatoes are fruit.) All that salsa and ketchup make tomatoes the most eaten fruit around the globe. Apples and bananas also rank at the top of the fruit tree.

Pomegranates, one of the less popular fruits today, were actually pretty popular in Bible times. The Old Testament contains twenty-five verses about this seed-filled, apple-looking fruit. The Bible explains that God wanted red, purple, and blue pomegranate decorations sewn onto the Israelite priest's garments with yarn (Exodus 28:33). King Solomon built his palace with pillars decorated with pomegranates (1 Kings 7:18–20). Check out these other fruit-filled verses:

- God's people remembered pomegranates grew in Egypt, and they longed for the tasty red fruit (Numbers 20:5).
- Israelite spies brought back pomegranates when they investigated the land of Canaan. In addition to the "milk and honey," the red fruit was a sign the land was good (Numbers 13:23).
- Solomon described his beautiful wife, saying her brow was "like a slice of pomegranate" (Song of Songs 6:7).

Further proving this fruit's popularity, archaeologists discovered a 3,000-year-old pomegranate in the Holy Land in 2018. Don't worry, it wasn't a really rotten, stinky piece of fruit covered in petrified mold. It was a clay pomegranate that was probably used as a table decoration, sort of like the ceramic pears and plastic apples people have today.

Whose table did this fruit adorn? Because it was discovered in Shiloh and dates back to a period when this city was the capital of Israel, archaeologists believe it belonged to a Jewish household.

Remember his covenant forever—the promise
he ordained for a thousand generations.
—1 Chronicles 16:15

DEFEND YOUR FAITH

The ancient Israelites were deeply spiritual people. Whoever owned the clay pomegranate probably held it as a reminder of God's provision and generosity. The pomegranate was one of the first symbols of God's people. According to tradition, pomegranates contain 613 seeds—which is the same number as commandments in the Torah (the first five books of the Bible). Many Jewish families eat pomegranates during festivals as a reminder of God's covenant.

The Bible contains many symbols of God's promises, such as a rainbow. During New Testament times, the cross, a dove, a fish, and a heart all became popular Christian symbols with special meanings.

Can you think of any symbols in your church or home that remind you of God's love? Maybe you could add a pomegranate as a reminder of God's generosity and how He always provides for you.

FUNNY FOODS

How would you like a big plate of fried tarantulas? If that's not your cup of tea, maybe you'd enjoy a bowlful of live octopus? No. Okay, how about just a cup of tea?

Some cultures eat strange-sounding foods. Of course, buffalo wings may sound weird to people outside of the United States. After all, buffaloes don't have wings.

Even common foods, such as pizza, get a funny twist in other countries. Although pepperoni is the topping of choice in the US, people in Japan often pick fish eggs or sweet corn. If you travel to Brazil, expect to see raw tuna and peas on your pizza. In India, minced mutton and pickled ginger are top sellers. A pizzeria in Belgium even puts grasshoppers, crickets, and worms on their pizzas.

More than 1,400 different types of insects appear on menus around the world. The most popular include locusts, beetles, termites, caterpillars, and bees. Bugs are often fried or dipped in chocolate. *Yum.* Or you can be like John the Baptist, who "ate locusts and wild honey" (Mark 1:6) in the wilderness.

The Old Testament lists locusts, grasshoppers, and crickets as good foods to eat. But lots of animals were off-limits (see Leviticus 11). Eating or even touching the meat or dead carcass of a camel, rabbit, pig, lizard, or lobster would make a person unclean.

Today, you can ingest all the "strange" food you want. But when you open your mouth to speak, make sure your words are clean.

"It's not what goes into the mouth that defiles a person, but what comes out of the mouth— this defiles a person."—Matthew 15:11

DEFEND YOUR FAITH

When Jesus came to earth, He shook things up. He told the people it's not what goes into your mouth that defiles you; it's what you say.

Bible teachers talk about the "old law" versus the "new law." In the Old Testament God's people were told to follow more than six hundred laws. That's a lot to remember. In the New Testament, Jesus said all those rules could be summed up in two commands: love God with all your heart, soul, and mind; and love your neighbor as yourself.

It might seem Jesus didn't like laws. That's not true. God gave the law to the people. Jesus even said that He didn't come to abolish the laws but to fulfill them (Matthew 5:17). Many Old Testament laws dealt with "earning" God's forgiveness through sacrifices or "gaining" God's favor through good actions. Through Jesus' sacrifice on the cross, God's forgiveness and favor are free gifts He gives us when we believe.

BE OF ONE MIND

Do you like to do a lot of things at once? Many kids listen to music, do their homework, text a friend, and eat a snack—all at the same time!

When we work on several things at once, we may think we're saving time. But researchers at a top university proved that when we try to do two things at once, we don't do a good job at anything.

The study looked at two sets of students. One group believed they were excellent multitaskers. They watched TV, held a conversation, and researched on the Internet all at once. The other group of students preferred to do one thing at a time. The research showed multitasking led to trouble. These students' brains tended to be more distracted and less able to memorize important information. But students who completed one task at a time could better remember and organize information. In test after test, the single-focused mind outperformed the multitasker.

God's Word doesn't contain any warnings about doing many things at once. But it does talk about having a singularly focused mind versus being *double-minded*. Being double-minded sounds like something a multitasker would want. But the term means lacking total trust in God. A double-minded person says they trust God, but they truly rely on themselves or things of this world. They don't fully give their hearts to God.

The Bible tells us to focus on one thing: God. In Matthew 6:33, Jesus said, "Seek first the kingdom of God and his righteousness, and all these things will be provided for you." God wants you to be single-minded. He wants—actually, He deserves—to be first in your life. Seeking God's kingdom should be your number one priority. But doing that can be difficult.

Draw near to God, and he will draw near to you. Cleanse your hands, sinners, and purify your hearts, you double-minded.—James 4:8

DEFEND YOUR FAITH

During no time in history have kids been so bombarded with information. A million (okay, probably not that many) distractions vie for our attention. There are smartphones, computers, video games, online media, schoolwork, sports schedules, and a bunch of other things buzzing around our brains.

With all the busyness, God can sometimes be pushed aside. Instead of giving God your leftovers at the end of the day or shooting up a few quick prayers to Him at mealtimes, strive to show Him how much you appreciate His love, mercy, and grace.

Jesus gave you a gift you can never repay. Don't be distracted. Focus your mind on Him, live in a way that honors Him, and then watch as He gives you everything you need.

WHY IS GOSSIP BAD?

Did you hear what Alyssa said about Brianna to Tyler and Lauren?"

If somebody ever asks you that question, you probably want to say, "No, and I don't want to hear it." Then walk away.

Most times when a conversation starts with "Did you hear?" it leads to gossiping. And gossip never leads to anything good.

Gossip occurs when you repeat a private story about another person. It can be real or made up. Sometimes people hear a juicy piece of news and start spreading it, even though the facts are wrong. Other times people get the story correct, but share it for the wrong reasons (such as to make themselves look good or to hurt the reputation of another person). Gossip is always hurtful, because it's always personal.

In the book of Romans, the apostle Paul listed sins that people commit when they don't follow God and turn to wickedness. Those sins include greed, hating God, envy, murder, quarreling . . . and gossip (Romans 1:29–31).

Some of those sins—like hating God and murder—seem really bad. But God puts gossip in the same category.

If you go to a big school or church, you know kids like to talk about each other. If you stand in a checkout lane at a grocery store and look at the magazines, you know that gossiping doesn't stop (in fact, it might get worse) when people get older.

Think about this: If a man farms a lot, he's called a farmer. If a girl dances all the time, she's called a dancer. But when someone spreads a lot of gossip, he's called a gossip—not a gossiper. Why?

The reason may be because gossip can take over your life and become who you are. Once you start to gossip, it's hard to stop. And that makes it very dangerous.

A contrary person spreads conflict,
and a gossip separates close friends.
—Proverbs 16:28

DEFEND YOUR FAITH

The next time you're tempted to pass along a piece of "news" you heard or share about somebody's personal life, think about the effect your words could have. Will they help the person you're talking about or hurt them?

If saying what you know to a teacher or adult helps the person or keeps others safe, it's not gossip. So if you see a student has brought a weapon to school or if you learn a friend is using illegal drugs, you need to tell someone.

The gossip the Bible warns about includes speaking behind each other's backs, spreading rumors, and telling others' secrets. That's something friends don't do.

Sometimes gossip can seem like it's no big deal; however, it's always a big deal to God.

God created the universe with natural laws. Our world has order. Nothing in creation happens by accident. Every plant, animal, force, and microscopic piece of matter obeys the laws that God set up.

Check out these ways to see God's orderly design.

• The planets travel around the sun in exact orbits. These orbits aren't perfect circles. The planets move in predictable, elliptical patterns. It takes Earth one year to travel around the sun. Mercury, the closest planet to the sun, makes its orbit in just three months. Neptune, on the other hand, takes almost 165 years to go around the sun once.

• Water is also predictable. It boils at 212 degrees Fahrenheit and freezes at 32 degrees. When water freezes, it forms six-sided crystals. If you look closely at a snowflake, you'll see it has six sides.

Throughout the Bible you can find many predictable patterns. One of those is *doing* and then *teaching* others about God.

Doing, or practicing and obeying God's laws, always comes before teaching others about Him. You can see it in the prophet Ezra and other Old Testament leaders. Even Jesus obeyed everything His Father and Scripture commanded before He taught others how to love God.

In the first verse of Acts, Luke, the author, explained that he wrote his Gospel about the things that Jesus "began to do and teach." Jesus taught His disciples to obey God's laws and said, "Whoever does and teaches these commands will be called great in the kingdom of heaven" (Matthew 5:19).

When the disciples returned to Jesus after sharing God's truth with the people, they excitedly reported to Jesus "all that they had done and taught" (Mark 6:30).

Now Ezra had determined in his heart to study the law of the Lord, obey it, and teach its statutes and ordinances in Israel.—Ezra 7:10

Defend Your Faith

Jesus wants us to be good teachers too. You can't teach someone how to shoot a basketball if you've never swished the ball through the hoop yourself. Similarly, you won't be able to really help people understand God and His ways if you don't know and obey them yourself.

When you are an active *doer*, you become more effective at being a *teacher* of those things. God wants you to obey Him. That's good for you for many reasons. One of them is so you can show and tell others how following God is always the right thing to do. God put everything in the universe in a specific order. Doing and then teaching is one of those God-ordained patterns.

MINDFUL OF THE MISTREATED

At a secret location in Iran, an amazing church gathered together. The pastor was sixteen years old. Most of the church members were between ten and thirteen.

They didn't play youth group games like trying to slurp baby food through a straw. They didn't do coloring sheets, watch the latest Christian videos, or get candy for memorizing Bible verses. These kids focused on becoming strong Christian leaders. Against many dangers, they learned how to talk about Jesus with Muslims, how to help new Christians, and how to start churches.

Iran is one of the hardest places in the world for people who love Jesus. Meeting together in a country where the official religion is Islam is risky.

At different times in history, Christians in Iran have been persecuted. But in the last twenty years, it's gotten worse. Believers in Jesus Christ have a tough time getting an education, holding a job, and owning a house.

Statistics show more than 260 million Christ followers in fifty countries are in danger of being put in prison or denied fundamental human rights because of their faith. Research also reveals that more Christians were killed for their belief in Jesus Christ during the last century than in every other century before that—combined.

Thousands of Christ followers will be killed for their faith this year. Those are serious and sad facts, but you can do something about it.

You may not feel persecuted for your faith. Maybe you get teased, but you probably don't fear being put in prison. The Bible tells us to remember our brothers and sisters in Christ who suffer for their beliefs. And that's exactly what you can do by praying for them. Prayer is more powerful than we may ever realize.

Remember those in prison, as though you were in prison with them, and the mistreated, as though you yourselves were suffering bodily.—Hebrews 13:3

DEFEND YOUR FAITH

Every year on the first Sunday in November, Christians around the world take part in the International Day of Prayer for the Persecuted Church. This is a day when families and churches pause and pray for the safety of fellow believers.

As part of God's body, we can pray that Christians will find comfort and encouragement in countries where they face persecution—North Korea, Afghanistan, Pakistan, and India are some of the worst. Pray for them to have courage and strength.

In the countries where living for Christ is the toughest, God is at work. Forty years ago in Iran, experts believe only around 500 Christians had converted from an Islamic background. Now the number of former Muslims who follow Jesus is estimated to be between 400,000 and a million people. Faithful believers, like the kids who met and continued to organize secret churches, are a big reason why.

A NAME TO REMEMBER

John Wauwaumpequunnaunt's last name was so hard to pronounce that even his English friends simply called him John. But what's not hard to understand is the impact he made for Christ in Colonial America.

When John was about thirteen, he'd often sneak away from his family's settlement in New York to visit a "praying town" in Stockbridge, Massachusetts. This praying town was started by the Puritans in 1739 to help Native Americans learn about Christianity.

As part of the Mohican tribe, John attended school in Stockbridge. At first John's parents didn't support his new education. They would bring him back to New York. But he protested so strongly that they eventually allowed him to live more than thirty miles from home.

Not only did John learn to read and write in English, but he also studied the Scriptures and became a Bible scholar. He was so smart and dedicated that the British missionaries recognized his gifts and asked him to help them reach out to his people.

When John was twenty years old, he helped missionaries David Brainerd and John Sergeant preach to the Mohicans. After Brainerd's death, another pastor came to Stockbridge. His name was Jonathan Edwards. With John's help, Edwards preached two hundred sermons to the Mohicans. Many of those sermons were published in books that scholars still read today. John also helped compile a dictionary so that the Bible could be translated in the language the Mohicans spoke.

Because John Wauwaumpequunnaunt studied diligently for translation work, many Native Americans heard the good news about Jesus in their own language. John dedicated his life to make sure his people learned about

Jesus. He was even chosen to run a school for other Native Americans. Yet, he stayed in the background to help others.

Be diligent to present yourself to God as one approved, a worker who doesn't need to be ashamed, correctly teaching the word of truth.—2 Timothy 2:15

DEFEND YOUR FAITH

In many ways, John was like a modern-day Barnabas, a man who helped the apostle Paul during his travels. Paul wouldn't have had as big an impact for God without Barnabas. But Paul's name is way more recognizable than Barnabas's.

God calls all kinds of workers to spread His truth. Some become famous for what they do for Christ. No matter what God calls you to do, work hard. Study God's Word so you know the truth. And don't back down when the opportunity to share about Jesus comes along.

John may not be as well known as the missionaries he helped, such as David Brainerd, John Sergeant, and Jonathan Edwards. But God knows his name—and He can even pronounce it!

DEFENDER FACTS
NAME: *JOHN WAUWAUMPEQUUNNAUNT*
PLACE: *MASSACHUSETTS*
TIME: *AROUND 1730–1764*

THE GOODNESS OF GOD

In the book of Mark, a rich young man ran up to Jesus and asked a really important question. "Good teacher," he said. "What must I do to inherit eternal life?" (10:17).

You'd think Jesus would answer clearly, saying that He is the way, the truth, and the life. Instead Jesus responded with a confusing question: "Why do you call me good? No one is good except God alone" (Mark 10:18).

Have you ever wondered, *Why would Jesus say that?*

- Is Jesus saying He's *not* good?
- Is He saying He's not *worthy* of being called good?
- Is He being overly humble and, in the process, confusing people as to who He really is?

The answer is . . . none of the above. Jesus loved the young man and wanted him to know the truth. But before Jesus answered, He wanted to make sure the man had his mind focused on God.

Notice how putting the emphasis on the wrong word can make Jesus' question confusing: "Why do you call *me* good?" Now read it with the emphasis on the first word: "*Why* do you call me good?"

Jesus knew the man wouldn't like the answer to the question. And before Jesus answered, He reminded the man who was talking to him. It's like Jesus was saying: "You just called Me good. Do you really believe that? Because only God is good. So if you believe I'm good, then you must believe I'm God. And if you realize I'm God, then you'll want to listen closely to the answer I give and be very careful to obey Me."

The LORD is good and upright; therefore he shows sinners the way.—Psalm 25:8

DEFEND YOUR FAITH

Over and over again the Bible confirms that God is good. Not only is God good, but He wants to rescue sinners. So when the man asked about inheriting eternal life, Jesus wanted to be especially clear. Jesus gave the man the same command He gave to the disciples and the same calling that He says to you: "Follow Me."

The man in the story didn't like Jesus' answer. Instead of putting Jesus above everything—including his money and possessions—and following God's Son, the man walked away.

When you read something Jesus said that seems confusing at first, ask God to help you figure it out. In addition to devotional books, like the one you're reading, Bible scholars have written books called *commentaries* that explain every passage in God's Word. As you read the Bible, always remember *who* is talking to you. Jesus is God in the flesh. When He tells you to do something, be sure to obey your good God for your own good!

EVIDENCE OF EXODUS

From the towering pyramids to the elaborate burial tombs in the Valley of the Kings, Egypt is a country rich with archaeological treasures. For years biblical archaeologists searched for evidence that this mighty, ancient kingdom was brought to its knees by the plagues described in the Old Testament.

In 1828, an interesting piece of papyrus was discovered in Egypt. The ancient plant-based "paper" was damaged and missing parts of the writing. Experts dated the document to around 1,500 to 1,300 BC. Then in 1909, Alan Gardiner, an Egyptologist, translated the papyrus that appeared to have been written by the Egyptian scribe Ipuwer.

In the form of a poem, Ipuwer described widespread plagues that line up remarkably well with the devastation in Exodus. These include: a river of blood (Exodus 7:20–21), the destruction of trees (9:23–25), groaning and wailing throughout Egypt (12:30), darkness in the land (10:22), and death (12:29–30). He said that in the chaos, the rich became poor and the poor became rich. All in all, Ipuwer detailed that Egypt had been laid to ruin.

The Bible explains how God's plagues came with a purpose. He wanted the Israelites to remember that He was their God (Exodus 6:6–8). But that wasn't all. God wanted the Egyptians to realize who He was too (7:5).

The Egyptians lived in a prosperous land with plenty of food and thousands of Israelite slaves to do hard work for them. The pharaoh was looked at as a god and commanded a powerful army. In the end, none of that mattered. God defeated Pharaoh so that all Egyptians would know He is Lord (Exodus 14:4, 16–18).

"You will know that I am the LORD your God, who brought you out from the forced labor of the Egyptians."—Exodus 6:7

DEFEND YOUR FAITH

Scholars continue to debate when the Ipuwer Papyrus was written and how literally it should be taken because it's in poetic form. Regardless, it's hard to argue how closely the descriptions of events line up with God's Word.

And one thing is for certain: The Bible makes it clear that God turned the Egyptians' way of thinking upside down. They believed in many "gods." They had a god of the Nile, god of earth, god of protection, and many others. Yet, when confronted by the one true God, the Egyptian gods were proven useless.

What brought fear and trembling to the Egyptians thousands of years ago can bring you strength and peace today. You can have confidence that you believe in the God of the universe. He is Lord of everything. The more you dig into the Bible—and the more archaeologists dig into biblical lands—the more evidence is found of that truth.

A group of cats is called a *clowder*.

A group of caterpillars is called an *army*.

A group of hippos is called a *thunder*.

A group of kangaroos is called a *mob*.

A group of Christians is called a *church*.

Going back to the original Greek word in the New Testament, a **church** is defined as an assembly of believers. Church isn't a building or an obligation. God's intent for the church was to bring His people together, not build massive structures.

What's the first word that comes to mind when someone says "church"?

Did you just think *boring*?

Be honest. Sadly, that's the first word that pops into a lot of kids' heads when they think about getting together with other believers.

Some estimates say more than 100 million Americans go to church on Christmas, which is the biggest day of the year for attendance. That sounds like a lot. However, over 100 million Americans watch the Super Bowl every year. Can you guess which activity is more important to God?

You're right. It's church. But which event generates more excitement?

Football fans act crazy. They go wild for their teams. Some fans paint their faces or whole bodies in their favorite team's colors before games. Then they scream and shout until their voices go out. They'll jump up and down. They'll stomp their feet. They know the statistics of all their favorite players.

That doesn't sound like church . . . but maybe it should.

He is also the head of the body, the church;
he is the beginning, the firstborn from the
dead, so that he might come to have first
place in everything.—Colossians 1:18

Defend Your Faith

As Christians we could learn something from sports fans. Not that we should do the wave in church or paint "J. C." on our cheeks before youth group (although that's not a bad idea). But we should be more excited about Jesus Christ. Jesus is the Head of the church. He gave everything for us. He defeated death. And He deserves to have first place in our lives.

We are part of God's body—His team. Now that's something worth cheering about. And it's something to learn more about through studying the facts and stats of our favorite Christian "players."

God's body isn't limited to a building. During a recent worldwide pandemic, churches weren't allowed to meet together. Buildings sat empty. But God's body stayed strong. The church even grew as more people turned to God to find a firm foundation for their lives.

So be excited about church. It's way better than being part of a crash of rhinos.

Can I Share My Faith at School?

Have you heard stories of kids getting in trouble for sharing their faith in Jesus at school? As unfair as it sounds, these reports are often true.

Maybe you've heard people say the separation of church and state *prevents* you from telling other students about Jesus. That's not true. The separation of church and state *protects* your legal right to live out your faith. But there's a right way to show your faith in school. For instance, in the United States:

• You have the right to pray silently or quietly before a test, your lunch, or whenever else you want to pray. You do not have the right to pray out loud whenever you want, especially when you're supposed to be quiet (like during a test).

• You have the right to talk about Jesus with other students at recess or in the lunchroom. You do not have the right to break school rules to tell others about God. Shouting in the library or talking about God when your teacher is speaking will get you into trouble.

• You have the right to read your Bible at school. You can read during free time, lunch, or recess. You don't have the right to read it when you're supposed to be doing schoolwork.

• You have the right to use Christian-themed notebooks and school supplies and to wear religious-themed clothing. But you can't break your school's dress code if it prohibits messages on clothes.

• You have the right to start a student-led Christian club. You just have to follow the same rules of other student-led clubs, such as having a teacher sponsor or meeting at specific times. You don't have the right to harass other students to join your club or to interrupt instruction time to tell others about the club.

"You will receive power when the Holy Spirit has come on you, and you will be my witnesses in Jerusalem, in all Judea and Samaria, and to the ends of the earth."
—Acts 1:8

DEFEND YOUR FAITH

Do all your rights to tell kids about Jesus at school surprise you?

When it comes to sharing the good news of Jesus, you have a lot of rights . . . and a lot of responsibilities. God wants you to be His witness close to home and spread out from there—and school is a great place to start.

When you tell others about Jesus *and* follow the laws, you become a powerful witness. Jesus said, "Give to Caesar the things that are Caesar's, and to God the things that are God's" (Mark 12:17). You shouldn't break the rules to share your faith. Know your rights; then live powerfully for God.

LIFE LESSONS FROM A LEPER

Have you ever watched a video of someone doing something klutzy and said to yourself, "I never want to do that!"? Or have you seen someone do something nice and said, "I really want to do that sometime"?

God gives us the ability to learn from the actions of people we see or read about. That's one of the many reasons He gave us the Bible. He wants us to learn lessons from the lives of people in His Word.

Leprosy was a terrible skin disease in Jesus' day. Anyone who had it wasn't allowed to be in contact with another person. No family. No church. No job. No friends. They couldn't touch or hug anyone. They were lonely and had almost no hope of being healed.

In the book of Luke, we read the story of Jesus meeting a group of ten lepers. They called out to Him, begging to be healed. Jesus felt compassion for the men and told them to go show themselves to the priests. They immediately started running to find a priest so they could make an offering. Even though they had not yet been healed, they trusted Jesus' command and believed He could cure them. As they ran, their leprosy disappeared. One of the men noticed his disease was gone. He turned around, ran back to Jesus, fell at His feet, and thanked Him.

Jesus looked at the man and said, "Were not ten cleansed? Where are the other nine? . . . Get up and go on your way. Your faith has saved you" (Luke 17:17–19).

Of the ten lepers, only one turned around to thank Him. This man's thankfulness was evidence of his faith and the best response to Jesus' miracle in his life.

Giving thanks always for everything to God the Father in the name of our Lord Jesus Christ.—Ephesians 5:20

DEFEND YOUR FAITH

Ten were healed. One came back, and he was blessed. That's a fact. It's also true that we often take God's blessings for granted. God deserves the glory and our thanks for everything He does for us.

The Bible says to give thanks to God for everything. That includes the prayers He answers—and the requests we have for God that He has yet to answer.

Go back to the story and notice how the lepers were healed as they ran, not before. Sometimes God wants us to obey Him before we know the final results. When we act in faith, it shows our trust in Him to always do what's best for us. That's why we can thank Him for His answers to our prayers even before He answers them.

So learn from the example of the grateful leper: trust Jesus, obey what He tells you to do, and then make sure to go back to Him and show your gratefulness.

HEAR NO EVIL

Noise. It can hurt your ears . . . and your life. Scientists say more than five million children ages six to nineteen suffer from noise-induced hearing loss.

God created your ears to be extremely sensitive. All the parts of your ear are intricately formed. Tiny bones, hairs, and tubes in your ears work in perfect coordination to allow you to distinguish sounds. You have 18,000 hairs in each ear, and all 18,000 could fit on the head of a pin! The two smallest muscles in your body are located in your ear. The bones, hairs, tubes, and muscles help you hear sounds as soft as zero decibels.

A whisper is around twenty decibels. Normal talking is sixty. Those noises won't damage your ears. But if sound levels reach more than 120 decibels, then hearing damage can occur in less than thirty seconds. It takes nearly two hours of exposure to sounds of ninety decibels to create hearing loss.

To figure out if a sound is dangerous, it's good to know that a typical hair dryer or lawn mower creates a noise of around ninety decibels. Ambulance sirens reach 120 decibels. And a jet plane (from one hundred feet away) makes sounds of more than 130 decibels.

Hearing loss is bad, but not hearing certain things can be good. Researchers say the greatest cause of hearing loss in kids is listening to loud music through headphones. And it's not just the sound that can be dangerous—the lyrics can also be harmful.

Some songs mock God or celebrate immoral behaviors, like abusing alcohol, using drugs, or being sexually active before marriage. God wants you to be careful about the messages you put into your mind from songs, TV shows, and movies. He wants you to protect your ears.

The time will come when people will not tolerate sound doctrine, but according to their own desires, will multiply teachers for themselves because they have an itch to hear what they want to hear. They will turn away from hearing the truth.—2 Timothy 4:3–4

DEFEND YOUR FAITH

The Bible warns of a time when people will turn away from hearing the truth. When you pray to accept Christ, you become a new creation, but your sinful nature doesn't go away. You're still tempted to sin. It's like you have two different voices whispering in your ears.

One voice tells you to listen to what you want—do what makes you feel good. The other voice encourages you to listen to God's truth and live for Him. When you fill your ears with messages that go against God's truth, it's easier to make compromises with your faith.

Being wise with what you allow into your ears is a daily battle. Protect your ears by listening to what is pure, lovely, true, and honorable (Philippians 4:8). These kinds of messages cut through the noise, build your faith, and help you do the right things.

PLAYING BY THE RULES

Our world is made up of rules. Police officers enforce them in neighborhoods. Referees enforce them in sports. Teachers enforce rules at school. Parents enforce them at home. God has rules that He must enforce too.

Very early in the Bible, two brothers brought an offering to God. They were the first two brothers. Abel brought an animal sacrifice, and God was pleased. His brother, Cain, brought fruit or vegetables, and God wasn't pleased (Genesis 4:2–5).

Many people read these verses and are confused. They think, *Why was God unfair and mean to Cain?*

Actually, God wasn't either of these things. He knew exactly what was going on. Cain wasn't playing by the rules. God's first rule always was—and always will be—love Him above all else. That means putting God above your possessions, your family, your comfort, and even your own life. God knew Cain had sin in his heart.

We can't know everything about Cain and Abel's sacrifice. But the Bible says Abel offered the firstborn of the flocks and the fat portions—that's the best of the best. Cain's offering is described as "some of the land's produce." Was it the best he had to give? Probably not.

Cain got really mad when God rejected his offering. God reminded him, "If you do what is right, won't you be accepted?" (Genesis 4:7). God is fair. By that statement, it's clear that Cain knew what was right . . . and God encouraged him to do the right thing. God wasn't going to bend His rules; Cain had to bend to follow God.

Cain didn't bend. He followed the wickedness in his heart and the results were devastating.

"But if you do not do what is right, sin is crouching at the door. Its desire is for you, but you must rule over it."—Genesis 4:7

DEFEND YOUR FAITH

God desired for Cain to do the right things and wanted to protect him from sin. But Cain got so angry that Abel's sacrifice had been accepted that he didn't "rule over" sin. He followed the path of sin. He murdered Abel. It was tragic, and Cain paid a terrible price because he pursued wickedness instead of living by God's rules.

God loves us and wants to protect us. He makes rules so we know the best way to live and the right way to treat others. God is never unfair or mean, so there's no justification in getting mad about God for His rules—like Cain did. If we don't live by God's rules, we often end up hurting ourselves or others.

Loving God above all else isn't confusing. The Bible says, "This is what love for God is: to keep his commands" (1 John 5:3). God loves you. Love Him back by obeying Him.

FROM FIGHTER TO FAITHFUL FOLLOWER

Columba, a dedicated monk, stood on one of Ireland's green hills. Below him lay a bloody battlefield. Some three thousand men had died. His warrior-clan's swords, axes, and spears had crushed the king's men. His family had won the fight, but Columba now realized the futility of war. He had fought to keep a Bible that he had copied by hand—a book of peace—through savage battle.

Around the year 560, Columba made a vow. He would seek three thousand men to convert to Christianity. This wouldn't amend for the senseless deaths from the battle he had fought, but it would keep him focused on God's work.

Three years later, Columba and twelve of his friends set out for Scotland, which was filled with fierce barbarians. The thirteen men settled on Iona, a small island off the coast. They built a modest community with huts, a library, a guesthouse, a kiln, a mill, two barns, and a small church.

At Iona, Columba trained missionaries to reach the people of Scotland. He and his followers sailed to the mainland, where they faced many dangers: savage people, wild animals, rugged terrain, and cold climate. There was another danger: the Druids. These pagan priests hated any messengers of Christianity.

Against these threats, Columba and his missionaries brought God's truth to Scotland. Columba was a large man with a booming voice who loudly sang praise songs to God to drown out the Druids' spooky chanting. He and his followers prayed for people and saw God answer mightily.

The light of God began to shine in a dark country. God blessed the missionaries' efforts of peacefully proclaiming the true gospel to a lost people.

Remind them . . . to obey, to be ready for every good work, to slander no one, to avoid fighting, and to be kind, always showing gentleness to all people.—Titus 3:1–2

DEFEND YOUR FAITH

At one time Columba was a selfish, angry person. He was willing to go to war over owning a Bible and defending his "rights." But God opened his eyes. Columba repented. He saw how his actions were not Christlike and loving. He changed and had a new priority: defending God's truth without fighting.

The Bible tells us to be ready for every good work. But we can't force anyone to believe in God. Instead of battling people to believe what we do, we are to be kind. When you avoid fighting and show gentleness, you reflect God's character. Fighting doesn't bring the fruit that God wants. You can accomplish much more through love, peace, patience, and kindness.

DEFENDER FACTS
NAME: *COLUMBA*
PLACE: *SCOTLAND*
TIME: *AROUND 521–597*

DON'T BEAR A GRUDGE

What's more dangerous: a bear, a shark, or a bee?

You might immediately think: *bear or shark*. With all of those teeth and claws, these animals look threatening. But worldwide, bear and shark attacks result in only about eight deaths a year.

Bees are far more dangerous. Because so many people are allergic to their stings, bees account for around one hundred fatalities each year. Although bees are harmful to some people, they're helpful to all people. Without bees pollinating plants, we'd have a lot less food to eat. Scientists estimate that bees pollinate about one-third of the food we consume.

Check out these other un-*bee*-lievable facts:

- A bee's buzz is created by its flapping wings that beat 11,400 times a minute.
- Honeybees can fly fifteen miles per hour.
- Honeybees may visit up to one hundred flowers during one trip before returning to their hive.
- Bees are the only insects that produce a food that's eaten by people.
- Between 20,000 and 60,000 bees can live in the same colony.
- Bees are great dancers. They dance to communicate with each other.

Although bears aren't that dangerous to humans, they are to bees. Bears love honey. They will often raid a beehive, eating the honey and the bees inside. That must make the bees want to bear a grudge.

"Do not take revenge or bear a grudge against members of your community, but love your neighbor as yourself; I am the LORD."
—*Leviticus 19:18*

DEFEND YOUR FAITH

The Bible doesn't have advice about bears, but it does have specific advice about not bearing a grudge.

A *grudge* is a strong feeling of anger or dislike toward someone that lasts a long time. Often when someone wrongs us, we want to get back at him. When we allow those feelings to linger, they can turn into a grudge.

Instead of holding on to a grudge, God wants us to offer forgiveness. Jesus even tells us in Matthew 5:39 to turn the other cheek when we're treated badly.

Seeking revenge is never a good plan. When we seek revenge, it only escalates the situation, and nobody wins. God tells us to leave revenge up to Him. By following God's advice, we can let go of past hurts and grudges, trust God to judge the wrongdoer, and go on with life.

Can you think of somebody who hurt you? Don't dwell on it. Instead ask God to give you the strength to forgive and love that person. Now that's the way to bee, *er . . .* be.

MORE PERMANENT THAN STONE

The book of Acts is filled with exciting stories of early church leaders spreading the truth about Jesus around the world. One of the most powerful missionary duos was Paul and Barnabas.

In Acts 13, they sailed to Cyprus to preach the gospel. As they traveled around the island, the Roman official Sergius Paulus became interested in their message. He asked Paul and Barnabas to meet with him. A sorcerer tried to prevent Paulus from hearing the Word of God. Paul wasn't scared. He looked at the sorcerer and said, "The Lord's hand is against you. You are going to be blind" (Acts 13:11). The sorcerer's eyes immediately went dark. When Paulus saw this, he believed in God.

Over the last couple hundred years, archaeologists have found evidence that adds credibility to this story. An inscription found on Cyprus in 1877 contained the title "proconsul Paulus." This inscription confirmed that Sergius Paulus really served as an official Roman proconsul during the time Paul and Barnabas were on the island.

Additionally, a memorial stone in Rome listed Paulus as an overseer. Historians believe this inscription dates to the first century, making it likely that it referred to the same man. Several inscriptions with the name L. Sergius Paulus have also been discovered near Pisidion Antioch. These either refer to the proconsul or his son, suggesting that the family estate might have been in the city.

These inscriptions confirm Sergius Paulus was a real person and reinforce the fact that Luke, the author of Acts, wrote about real people and real events.

You show that you are Christ's letter, delivered by us, not written with ink but with the Spirit of the living God—not on tablets of stone but on tablets of human hearts.—2 Corinthians 3:3

DEFEND YOUR FAITH

Words carved in stone give us an amazing ability to look back in time and learn about people, traditions, and histories that would be lost if they had been written on paper or not recorded at all. Just like in the case of Sergius Paulus, stone inscriptions have corroborated stories from the Bible.

When God made His covenant with the Israelites, He wrote His law on stone tablets that were placed in the ark of the covenant (Exodus 31:18). Ultimately, God knew from the beginning that the old covenant wouldn't be enough. Stone lasts a long time, but it eventually breaks down.

Instead of writing the law on stone tablets, God now writes His teachings on our hearts through His Son (Jeremiah 31:33 and 2 Corinthians 3:3). Everything in this world will fade away. Our lives are the new evidence of God's power and truth. Through His followers, God's new covenant is way more permanent than stone.

WHAT WILL HAPPEN WHEN JESUS RETURNS?

Have you ever seen a sci-fi or superhero movie where characters strap on a jetpack and zoom around the world? Other characters in these films may have the ability to disappear from one place and appear in another to avoid danger.

God has a similar plan for His believers when Jesus returns. Only God doesn't need sci-fi technology, and it will happen much faster than a jetpack.

The Bible contains numerous passages about what's going to happen in the future. Even in the Old Testament, it was clear that God would return and redeem His creation. Jesus spoke about coming again and appearing in the sky (Matthew 24:30). And the apostle Paul wrote about how believers in Christ would meet Jesus in the air (1 Thessalonians 4:17).

As Christians, we can eagerly wait for Jesus to come down and take us to be with Him for all eternity. He will change all living believers to have bodies that can't be hurt, won't die, and are designed to live forever in God's presence. Some Christians refer to this great moment as the *rapture*. The word comes from a Latin translation of the term "carry off," and it means to snatch away something very quickly.

When Jesus returns, the Bible says we will hear a heavenly shout. Maybe it'll be the words, "Come up here!" Then Jesus and His angels will take us home with Him. It won't be a scary moment. It'll be more like your mom saying, "Come home for dinner," and you will joyfully look up to see Him coming.

We will be caught up together . . . to meet the Lord in the air, and so we will always be with the Lord.—1 Thessalonians 4:17

DEFEND YOUR FAITH

Nobody knows exactly when Jesus will return—not even Him (Mark 13:32). Really smart Bible experts have studied the book of Revelation and other passages in the Old and New Testament about the end times. A lot of scary stuff will happen in the future—wars, natural disasters, and a rise of evil. Things are going to get worse before they get better.

The Bible doesn't talk about the end times to frighten you. God's Word contains signs and warnings as a wake-up call to His people. He wants us to be ready. What's more, these passages should give you peace. Jesus wins in the end. The Devil is defeated. God creates a new heaven and earth, and believers live forever with Him in paradise.

Jesus' return is nothing to fear; it's actually something to look forward to. And if you think flying around with a jetpack would be cool, just wait till Jesus beams you up to be with Him!

SMILE AWHILE

Babies are born with the ability to smile. From the beginning, God created us to smile. Doctors have even proven with 4D ultrasound technology that babies smile in the womb *before* they are born. And once they're born, they smile a lot. Children often smile around four hundred times a day, which is way more than adults.

Scientists have tried to determine whether it's harder to smile or frown. (Yes, these scientists have too much time on their hands.) Basically, it takes the same number of muscles to make each facial expression—twelve for smiling, eleven for frowning. But since we smile more than frown, it's actually easier to smile because those facial muscles are stronger.

Researchers have found another very important fact about smiles: They're contagious. Numerous studies have shown that humans mirror the expression on a face they're looking at. One study revealed when people looked at a photo of somebody smiling, they smiled too. And here's the best part. Not only did they smile, but they felt better. Their mood changed, and they felt more confident about tackling a challenge. Even people who were told to smile started feeling happier than their non-smiling counterparts once their frowns turned upside down.

Isn't it cool that smiles don't just spread happiness to other people, they spread happiness inside of us too?

King Solomon probably wasn't trying to be scientific when he wrote that a joyful heart makes you smile. But science has proven it's true: You wear your feelings on your face. When you're happy, it shows.

A joyful heart makes a face cheerful,
but a sad heart produces a broken spirit.
—Proverbs 15:13

DEFEND YOUR FAITH

As Christ followers we have a lot of reasons to smile. We know God personally. We know we're forgiven. We know God hears us and answers prayers. We know God sent the Holy Spirit to help us walk with Him. We know we'll live forever with God. If our facial expressions aren't positive, we're not displaying the joy we have through Jesus.

Try this experiment right now. Go to a mirror and smile at yourself. How did it make you feel? A little happier, right?

Now the next time you're at church or school, smile at someone, and see what happens. Not only can you smile, but you can also notice if a friend isn't smiling. It may mean her heart is sad or something is bothering her. Talk to her to show you care, and try to cheer her up.

God created smiles to have positive power. They draw people to you, spread happiness, and better express the joy God brings to your life. So smile awhile and see what God does through you.

THE POINT OF THE BIBLE

Some people think the Bible is just a bunch of rules. And it's true; God's Word is filled with His commands on how to live:

- Don't lie.
- Don't steal.
- Do honor your parents.
- Don't be jealous of your friend's stuff.
- Do get together with other believers.
- Don't think bad things about people.
- Don't murder.

There's a lot more too. But the Bible wouldn't be the best-selling book ever written if it were just a list of rules. That would be boring. The Bible is anything but boring. It's filled with poetry and interesting people, battles and betrayals, relationships and revelations.

Sure, plenty of verses provide tips on how to live successfully and serve God. But the whole purpose of the Bible is to point to Jesus. He's the main character. Every book points us to God's Son, who came to rescue us from sin and restore our relationship with the heavenly Father. The Bible isn't about us and what we should do. The Scriptures tell God's story—what He has done through His Son, and what will happen because of Jesus in the future.

Jesus Himself made this point when He was talking with the religious leaders in John 5. Many of these men had memorized massive amounts of Scripture. They thought they had to know and follow all of God's laws to earn their way to heaven. Jesus set them straight.

"You pore over the Scriptures because you think you have eternal life in them, and yet they testify about me."—John 5:39

DEFEND YOUR FAITH

Forgiveness and eternal life don't come through knowing the Scriptures. Eternal life comes only from knowing Christ. God's Word points to Jesus because forgiveness comes only by believing in Him.

Quick quiz: Where can you find the verse that says, "For God loved the world in this way: He gave his one and only Son, so that everyone who believes in him will not perish but have eternal life"?

You may immediately recognize that as John 3:16. Bible experts say it's the most quoted and well-known verse in the Bible. Do you know why? It's because John 3:16 summarizes the entire purpose of the Bible. Without Jesus, there is no forgiveness. Without Jesus, we can't have a personal relationship with God. Without Jesus, there's no reason for the Bible.

So next time you read God's Word, don't think of it as a bunch of rules. It's the story of God's love for His creation. All sixty-six books point to Jesus because God knew we'd need a lot of reminding about His forgiveness and love.

UNDER OATH

Swearing is bad. And not just when it comes to cuss words. Jesus warned us not to swear an *oath*.

The word **oath** is a vow that means you will fulfill a promise. It's a guarantee that you'll do what you say. In Old Testament times, people would make an oath by saying, "I swear by heaven that this [insert promise] will happen." When you bring up God or heaven in an oath, that's serious business.

Even in the New Testament, Jesus took oaths seriously. He wanted His followers to speak the truth and act with integrity. In other words, our actions and words should be consistent with our values and beliefs. He didn't want us to make promises we couldn't keep.

As Christians sometimes we can feel obligated to say yes when we see opportunities to help.

- "Yes, I'll help tutor after school."
- "Yes, I'll play on the youth group worship team."
- "Yes, I'll mow the neighbor's yard."
- "Yes, I'll make cookies for the bake sale."

Saying yes feels good. It can make us popular and helps other people. Besides, that's what Jesus would want us to say, right?

Not always.

If we say yes to too many things, we can become over-committed and start dropping the ball. Being busy and helping others is definitely a good thing. But being over-whelmed with responsibilities can lead to feeling stressed, sick, and tired.

When we back out of a commitment, fail to follow through on a promise, or do a project that reflects less than our best (just to get it done), it doesn't look good. People may start to look at us and think we're flakey—not faithful. There's a reason Jesus said, "Let your 'yes' mean 'yes,' and your 'no' mean 'no.'"

"But let your 'yes' mean 'yes,' and your 'no' mean 'no.' Anything more than this is from the evil one."—Matthew 5:37

Defend Your Faith

Before you say yes to something, check your motivations. Are you doing it to please people or to please God? Make sure you're using your time and talent on things God has called you to do. Saying no isn't fun, but sometimes it helps you live a more powerful life for God.

In court cases, people swear an oath to always tell the truth. Similarly, your parents, teachers, and friends should be able to trust what you say. If you say yes, make sure you have time to do your best. If you're too busy or not totally committed, don't feel bad about saying no.

Think about the things you've promised to people. Is there an "oath" you need to follow through on? Living with integrity earns people's respect . . . and reflects well on your belief in Christ.

GOD'S MOUTHPIECE

Do you suffer from *glossophobia*?

Moses might have. Glossophobia is just a fancy way of saying you're afraid to speak in public. Research shows that speech anxiety is in the top ten of fears worldwide. Others on the list include the fear of spiders, the fear of lightning, and the fear of elevators.

When God called Moses to go back to Egypt and lead the Israelite slaves to freedom, Moses told God that He'd picked the wrong man. He wasn't famous or powerful, and he didn't speak that well. Actually, Moses' exact words were "my mouth and my tongue are sluggish" (Exodus 4:10).

Maybe Moses had recently eaten too many hot peppers. Those will make your mouth numb. But it's more likely that Moses was scared and making excuses.

God wasn't having any of it. He got angry. He told Moses that He'd help Moses speak and teach him what to say. God even sent along Moses' brother, Aaron, to help him talk to Pharaoh.

With God and his brother at his side, Moses became one of the greatest leaders of all time. He led the Israelites out of Egypt, parted the Red Sea, received the Ten Commandments, brought forth water from a rock, and led God's people to the doorstep of the Promised Land.

Moses was brave. After a brief argument with God, He trusted the Lord to lead him. He kept his mind focused on God and found the courage to do something that nobody had done in four hundred years—free God's people from slavery! Because of Moses' faith, he witnessed God's miracles and watched God fulfill His promise to deliver His people.

"Now go! I will help you speak and I will teach you what to say."—Exodus 4:12

Defend Your Faith

Is God asking you to trust Him and step out in faith? He probably won't ask you to do something like speak to a powerful world leader and walk through a massive body of water. But it may be new and scary to you. He can help you be brave in whatever He's calling you to do.

Stepping out for God is never easy. You may be nervous if you feel God is asking you to do something outside of your comfort zone. Moses probably would've agreed right away if God asked him to tend sheep. But God told Moses to speak for Him! Talk about having a lot of responsibility.

If you're afraid to do something for God, ask Him to help you. Moses kept following God, kept talking, and kept walking. He looked to God to lead him, and you can do the same.

Defender Facts
Name: *Moses*
Place: *Egypt*
Time: *Around 1500–1380 BC*

BLOWING UP THE TRUTH

The Islamic State in Iraq and Syria, known as ISIS, has done terrible things in recent times. They've kidnapped children, killed thousands of people, planned terrorist attacks, held thousands of people as slaves, and destroyed valuable historical sites and objects.

In 2014, ISIS destroyed many historical artifacts and sites in Mosul, Iraq, including a shrine to the prophet Jonah. Once Mosul (which had been the ancient city of Nineveh) was recaptured by Iraqi security forces in 2017, archaeologists from around the world began looking in the deep underground tunnels of the city.

They soon found an ancient palace built for Assyrian King Sennacherib and later possibly expanded by his son Esar-haddon. Although ISIS had taken smaller artifacts that could be sold, inscriptions were found in an old city wall that listed Assyrian kings in the order of which they ruled: Sargon, Sennacherib, Esar-haddon, and Ashurbanipal. That's the exact same order that the Bible records their reigns: Sargon (Isaiah 20:1); Sennacherib (2 Kings 18–19); Esar-haddon (2 Kings 19:37); Ashurbanipal (Ezra 4:10).

Two of those kings played an interesting role in Israel's history. In 2 Kings 18, King Sennacherib attacked and captured many cities in Judah. The Assyrian king was confident that his vast army would soon destroy Jerusalem. The king of Judah, King Hezekiah, cried out to God for help (2 Kings 19:14–19). The prophet Isaiah informed the distraught king that the Lord's hand was against Assyria. That night an angel of the LORD struck down thousands of Assyrian warriors. King Sennacherib returned to Nineveh, where he was assassinated by his family and succeeded by his son Esar-haddon.

King Hezekiah knew what the Assyrian kings were unable to figure out: God alone establishes kingdoms and removes kings (Daniel 2:21).

LORD our God, please save us from his power
so that all the kingdoms of the earth may
know that you, LORD, are God—you alone.
—2 Kings 19:19

DEFEND YOUR FAITH

King Hezekiah recognized his complete dependence on God. The battle wasn't Hezekiah's to win. Victory or defeat wouldn't rest with his ability as a leader and fighter. Victory could only come from the power of God.

Although the Assyrian kings believed themselves to be powerful rulers, in the end their kingdoms fell to ruin and disrepair. Dirt covered once-grand palaces. Their names are remembered only as kings from long ago.

God and His promises, on the other hand, endure forever. As King David wrote in Psalm 145:13, "Your kingdom is an everlasting kingdom; your rule is for all generations."

ISIS meant to destroy history. Instead more truth was dug up to prove the accuracy of the Bible. Once again, archaeology demonstrated the historical accuracy of the Bible as a whole—and the fact that only God's kingdom will go on forever.

DOES GOD FORGIVE AND FORGET?

What's your earliest memory? Most people can't remember anything before they were three years old. How far can you think back?

Every night when you sleep, your mind organizes the events of the day, stores memories, and discards other stuff. But as awesome as your mind's ability to remember is, it can't remember everything. Some memories fade. Your short-term memory, which keeps track of what's happening now, can only store about seven items at a time. That means a lot of information gets lost.

Not all memories are created equal. When someone hurts you, it tends to stick. Your parents might tell you to "forgive and forget." But does that really work? You might be able to forgive a friend right away, but forgetting what they did takes time.

So how does that work with God? Does He really forget our sins?

Because God is "omniscient," which means He knows absolutely everything, He *can't* forget our sins . . . or anything else. The Bible never says that God will "forgive and forget" our wrongdoings. But numerous verses point out that God will remember our sins no more (see Isaiah 43:25, Hebrews 10:17, and Jeremiah 31:34).

There's a difference between *forgetting* and *not remembering*. When you remember something, you bring it to mind. You think about it and replay what happened. You may not be able to forget that a friend hurt you with something she said, but you don't have to keep bringing it back to mind. And if it does come to mind, you can stop thinking about it and think of something else—like how your friend apologized to you.

That's sort of the way it works with God. And He's way better at *not* remembering!

"I will forgive their iniquity and never again remember their sin."—Jeremiah 31:34

Defend Your Faith

God promises that He will not bring your sins to mind and hold them against you for all eternity. And when God makes a promise, He keeps it.

Your sins hurt God. He loves you as His child and calls you His friend. Just like your friends can hurt you deeply, God feels the same way when we sin against Him. When we choose to disobey God, it's like we're telling Him, "You don't mean that much to me."

As a human it'd be hard to forget that. But because of the forgiveness we have through our faith in Jesus, God chooses not to remember. The Bible says, "If we confess our sins, he is faithful and righteous to forgive us our sins and to cleanse us from all unrighteousness" (1 John 1:9). God makes us clean. He forgives. When God forgives, He *can't* forget—but He *won't* remember. That's a great example of true forgiveness.

LEARN TO BE A LOGGER

Forests cover about one-third of the earth's land. The heaviest living organism in the world is an aspen tree. Well, *trees*. Quaking aspens branch off from a single tree and share a root system. This aspen grove, called Pando, covers more than one hundred acres in Utah and weighs an estimated 13 million pounds. That's one big creation from an even more amazing Creator.

God made trees to provide oxygen, shade, a home for animals, and building materials. Plus, they're beautiful and a perfect place for a tree house!

More than thirty types of trees are mentioned in the Bible, including gopher wood. That's what Noah cut down to build the ark. Today, the men and women who cut down trees are called lumberjacks. Their work can be hard and dangerous, so they wear hard hats, gloves, and protective glasses.

Similarly, removing "logs" from our lives takes effort. In Luke 6:37–42, Jesus used a logging analogy to explain the downfall of judging others. Jesus told His followers, "Do not judge, and you will not be judged." Then He said we all have a tendency to point out the speck in somebody else's life while missing the log that's messing up our own lives. Jesus' advice? Be a logger.

When some people read "do not judge," they think it means we should accept everyone and never tell others that what they're doing is wrong. That's not what Jesus says. He wants us to be discerning, which means to show good judgment. If a friend is using drugs, stealing, or lying, it's okay to tell them that's not okay.

At the same time, Jesus wants us to look at our lives before telling others how to live. Sometimes a "log" blocks our ability to give good advice. If we copy a friend's homework, but then tell them not to peek at our paper during a test, it's hypocritical. Both copying *and* peeking are cheating.

"First take the beam of wood out of your eye, and then you will see clearly to take out the splinter in your brother's eye."—Luke 6:42

DEFEND YOUR FAITH

God knows that by removing the beam in your life, you're better able to help others. As you look at your life, what are some areas where you could become more like Jesus? Maybe you're sarcastic. Perhaps you're not as helpful as you could be. Come up with a mental list.

Now think like a lumberjack, and start chopping. You may experience a little pain, but God will walk with you to become more like Him.

Once you can see clearly, you'll be able to help remove the splinters from your friend's eye and better see God's plans for your life.

GETTING TO THE ROOT OF PERSEVERANCE

What do you call someone who starts an 800-meter race but decides to run just one lap?

A quitter.

That may sound harsh, but it's true. When you compete in the 800 meters, the goal is to complete *two* full laps as fast as possible. If you quit halfway because you're breathing hard, then you're not showing the perseverance needed to finish the race.

The word *perseverance* doesn't show up much in the Bible, but you probably hear a lot about it from your parents and at church. It means to maintain your Christian faith through trying times. As believers in Christ, we need to remain faithful to God in the face of opposition and discouragement.

Jesus compared people who hear and accept His truth to seeds that were spread on the ground (see Matthew 13). If a seed rooted and started to grow, one of three things happened:

> 1. It sprouted up quickly. But it didn't grow deep roots in the rocky soil, and the heat caused it to wither.
> 2. It grew up only until the thorns and weeds choked it.
> 3. It sprouted up in good soil, grew deep roots, and produced fruit.

The seeds that showed perseverance by growing deep roots thrived. Sadly, the seeds that faced opposition from weeds and discouragement from a rocky, heated environment didn't make it.

We desire each of you to demonstrate the same diligence for the full assurance of your hope until the end, so that you won't become lazy but will be imitators of those who inherit the promises through faith and perseverance.—Hebrews 6:11–12

DEFEND YOUR FAITH

As the early church started to grow, followers of Jesus faced a lot of persecution. Some people chose to fall away from God instead of persevering. Living out the Christian faith wasn't easy back then, and it's not easy today.

Many of God's standards go against popular culture. Maybe you've seen a kid who gets surrounded by thorny friends and has his faith choked out. Similarly, people who don't put down deep roots could have their faith wither and die. To persevere in your relationship with Christ, you have to put down deep roots.

Running the race for Christ takes endurance (see Hebrews 12:1) and being rooted to God requires effort. Sitting on the couch doesn't create faithfulness. Reading the Bible, learning about your beliefs at church, seeking the truth, and praying to God does.

Don't allow attacks on your beliefs to stop you from growing into the person God has planned for you to be. The root of perseverance is faithfulness. So stay faithful and don't quit—in a race or in your relationship with God.

GOD'S GIFT TO THE WORLD

What's the best gift you've ever received? A new bicycle? Some cool shoes? A puppy? A bag of gold?

A bag of gold could come in handy. That was one of the gifts the wise men brought to baby Jesus in Bethlehem. We don't know exactly how many wise men visited Jesus, but we do know they brought Him three precious gifts: gold, frankincense, and myrrh. Have you ever wondered, *Why these gifts and not a stuffed sheep?*

Gold is one of the world's most precious metals. It represents power, wealth, and purity in the Bible. Gold is a sign of a king's riches. Jesus was the King of kings. The inside of the Holy of Holies, the most sacred place in the Jewish temple that was dedicated to God, was completely covered with gold. The gift of gold was a gift fit for Jesus the King.

Frankincense is a sweet incense that was part of a special mixture used by priests as a fragrance for worship. This mixture was not to be used by the people for personal use, but only by priests as they served God in the temple. Frankincense was a gift fit for Jesus the High Priest.

Myrrh, a spice, was used as the main ingredient in the anointing oil that was sprinkled on the temple altar, furnishings, and the priests. In the Old Testament, myrrh was applied to dedicate someone to God's service. The New Testament describes how myrrh was used to anoint bodies for burial. Myrrh was a gift fit for Jesus the Anointed One, which is the meaning of the word *Christ*.

The gifts of the wise men are a great example of how many of the simple facts in Scripture have much deeper meanings.

*The wages of sin is death, but the gift of God
is eternal life in Christ Jesus our Lord.
—Romans 6:23*

DEFEND YOUR FAITH

The gifts of the wise men showed great honor to Jesus. But they don't compare to the gifts God gives us. God is the greatest gift-giver ever. James 1:17 says, "Every good and perfect gift is from above, coming down from the Father of lights."

Everything you have comes from God. The family you live with, your home, your talents and abilities, your possessions— all of it comes from God. But the best gift that God offers to everyone who trusts in Jesus as Savior is the gift of eternal life. We can't do anything to earn God's favor because of our sin. And we don't have to, because God offers forgiveness and salvation as a gift.

Take a moment to thank God and to think of someone in your life you would like to tell about this wonderful free gift from God—the ultimate gift-giver!

MAKE A RIPPLE EFFECT

Have you ever skipped a rock across a lake? With each skip, ripples move out in circles from where the rock hit the water. These little circles get bigger and bigger.

What's your best "skip"? Three times? Seven? The world's best stone skippers can zip a rock so it skips nearly ninety times! That's a lot of ripples.

Scientifically speaking, a "ripple effect" is created by adding energy to the surface of the water. When the rock hits the water, it "pushes" water out of the way and creates a splash of energy. This energy then travels away from the point of impact in the form of ripples.

God created nearly all energy to move in waves. Waves in the ocean are created by wind energy. Sound moves in waves; so does light energy. The ripples on the water are actually energy waves. The bigger the rock that hits the water, the more energy it creates, and the bigger the ripples.

Jesus was a big Rock (1 Corinthians 10:4). His death and resurrection created a ripple effect that's still being felt today.

The book of Acts shows how Jesus' followers grew from a small number of believers in Jerusalem to a worldwide movement. In Acts 1:8, Jesus told His disciples that the Holy Spirit would give them power, and they would be witnesses of His resurrection to people in Jerusalem, in all of Judea and Samaria, and finally to the "ends of the earth."

If you look at a map, Jerusalem was where Jesus died on a cross and rose from the dead—that's where the Rock hit the water. Judea and Samaria were first to feel the ripple in the next regions over. The disciples kept teaching about Jesus as His power, and the energy from His Word made ripples throughout the entire world.

The word of God spread and multiplied.
—Acts 12:24

Defend Your Faith

The truth of salvation in Jesus spread out from Jerusalem like a rock landing in a pond. This ripple effect continues today through disciples like you! Jesus wants you to go and tell the world about God's love for them (Matthew 28:19–20).

Your actions have a ripple effect. Think of what you do as "stones" you throw that send ripples out to other people. When you show kindness to a neighbor by bringing in their garbage cans, you spread God's love. When you invite a friend to church so she can hear the truth about Jesus, God's power starts to move. God wants everybody to know how much He loves and cares for them. That happens when we're faithful to tell people what God has done in our lives and share what we know about the truth in the Bible.

Just think about what a great ripple effect you can make in the world for Jesus!

On the day of Jesus' resurrection, He walked with two men from Jerusalem to the city of Emmaus (see Luke 24:13–35). These men knew Jesus, but they were "prevented from recognizing" Him during the journey. As they walked, they discussed everything that had just happened. The men believed Jesus was the Messiah, so they couldn't understand why He had been sentenced to death and crucified. Even more surprising, they'd heard from some women that Jesus' body was gone! Jesus stayed with the men, explaining what His teachings meant. He even had dinner with them—before opening their eyes to the fact they were with the risen Lord.

For centuries, archaeologists have searched for the location of Emmaus. The biblical account and other references establish that this city was located seven miles from Jerusalem; however, the exact location of Emmaus seemed lost to history. But after excavations in a town known as Kiriath-Jearim in 2019, archaeologists believe they've discovered new evidence that pinpoints Emmaus' location.

Kiriath-Jearim is seven miles from Jerusalem. It has remains of fortified walls and what might have been a tower that dated back before Rome conquered the region. During the four hundred years between the end of the Old Testament and when Jesus was born, towns outside of Jerusalem were fortified to form a ring of protection. The Jewish historian Josephus provides a list of these towns, most of which have been identified. However, Kiriath-Jearim isn't on the list. Emmaus is. Archaeologists now suggest that Kiriath-Jearim and the neighboring town, Abu Gosh, are together what Josephus and the Gospel writer Luke referred to as Emmaus.

Archaeologists continue to look for additional evidence, such as an inscription, to positively identify the city. But these recent discoveries certainly point to a location where the newly risen Savior walked and taught.

*"The Counselor, the Holy Spirit,
whom the Father will send in my name,
will teach you all things and remind you of
everything I have told you."—John 14:26*

DEFEND YOUR FAITH

Sometimes we might have trouble seeing what God is doing, even if it's right in front of us. Our emotions can get in the way. If we're mad or sad, it might obscure God's work and presence in our lives. But God doesn't want us to wander down a road, feeling confused and alone—like the men did on the road to Emmaus. Because the truth is, we're never alone.

When Jesus ascended back into heaven, He sent the Holy Spirit. Just like Jesus opened the men's eyes, God's Spirit reminds us of the hope we have in Christ and gives us fresh insights from His Word.

We won't always see how God works in this life, but the Holy Spirit can help us navigate the pain, uncertainty, and confusion we sometimes experience. His Spirit walks along the road with us, even when we can't see He's there.

WHAT'S WRONG WITH WANTING FAME?

What do you want to be when you grow up?

When your parents were asked that question as children, the popular answers back then were doctor, professional athlete, teacher, veterinarian, and police officer. According to a recent survey, doctor still tops the list. But the second-most sought-after job mentioned by kids is *social media influencer*. The reason? Money and fame.

Online video platforms have made it possible for people to be famous for being famous. People post anything online in hopes of hitting the big-time: cute cats, playful babies, funny dances, opening toys, crazy trick shots. According to statistics, one hundred hours of video are uploaded on YouTube every minute.

Most of these videos will receive fewer than fifty views. Only two percent will break the 1,000 mark. A tiny fraction of one percent will reach 500,000 views. Those statistics are pretty sad. And without millions of views and advertising sponsors, the money most videos generate is sad too. The truth is, fame on social media is pretty fleeting.

Wanting to be famous is nothing new. The Bible tells about a man who claimed to be somebody great by using magic. In the book of Acts, Philip met a sorcerer named Simon. Simon heard Philip preach about God, believed in Jesus (Acts 8:13), and started following Philip around. Soon Peter and John arrived in Samaria and prayed for the new believers to receive the Holy Spirit. When Simon saw the power of the Holy Spirit, he offered Peter and John money for the ability to touch people and have them receive God's Spirit.

Immediately, Peter told Simon that God's gifts can't be bought. And because Simon's heart wasn't right, Peter added that Simon wouldn't be able to minister for God.

Many live as enemies of the cross of Christ.
Their end is destruction; their god is their
stomach; their glory is in their shame; and
they are focused on earthly things.
—Philippians 3:18–19

DEFEND YOUR FAITH

Simon was a magician. He was used to being famous. When he witnessed the power of the Holy Spirit, he saw a pathway to greater fame.

Fame is the aim of many people today. The Bible warns against this mindset, saying not to set your mind on earthly things and glory in your shame. Instead of posting videos of yourself falling down or getting injured (hoping to grow your own name), seek to honor God in everything you do and say. Fame lifts *you* up. Your life should lift up God's name. If you seek to make God famous—and not yourself—you'll be sharing a name that lasts way longer than fifteen minutes.

AS GOOD AS IT GETS

What are your goals for the future? Do you want to learn to play the piano, travel the world, or become a computer programmer?

Reaching a goal always has two parts: the goal and the way to get there.

Did you know that God has a goal for all believers? It's for us to be good. But make sure you have the understanding of the word *good*.

Good is often defined as the opposite of bad. In this way of thinking, if you do more good things than bad things, then you're good. Others think *good* is a desired quality, such as wanting to have a good life or attend good schools.

God doesn't see this word that way. His definition of *good* is to be more like Jesus. That's the goal. And He has some pretty creative ways to help us get there. God often uses trials—such as hardships, troubles, and dealing with mean people—to mold us into being more like His Son. Jesus dealt with all those things when He was on earth. We can read about what He did and learn from His example. He forgave those who mistreated Him. He prayed when trouble came. He relied on God's strength and God's Word to get through hardships. When He had a decision to make, He always did whatever would please God (John 8:29).

We know that all things work together for the good of those who love God, who are called according to his purpose . . . to be conformed to the image of his Son.—Romans 8:28–29

DEFEND YOUR FAITH

Romans 8:28–29 tells us when we love God that *all* things work out for good, which means we become more like Jesus. No matter what happens—in the best and worst times—the goal is for us to conform more into the image of His Son. When we do well, God wants us to be thankful to the people who helped us. When people are mean to us, He wants us to trust God and forgive them. Whenever we do what pleases God in a hard situation, it changes our heart to be more like Jesus.

Goals are sometimes hard to reach. This one is especially tough. You'll never be exactly like Jesus while you're on earth. But you can make it a goal to become more like Jesus every day. Think more of others than yourself. Put others' needs above your own. During your lifetime, God wants you to resemble Jesus in the way you make decisions and how you love God and others.

Being like Jesus is as good as it gets!

NEW WORLD, NEW START

When William Bradford was twelve years old, he followed some friends to a church ten miles from his family's farm. William had always attended the Church of England. His uncles took him every Sunday after his parents died. But the church in Scrooby was different. The people closely studied the Scriptures and allowed him to ask questions.

At this point in history, King James I wanted everyone to join the Church of England. People who didn't join were often thrown in jail and persecuted. William and his church friends, called *Separatists*, were mistreated. By 1608, they'd had enough. They left England and moved to the Netherlands to find a place where they could freely worship God.

After twelve years in the Netherlands, some members of the Scrooby group—and a few others—decided to move to the New World, where they could worship as they pleased. William and his wife, Mary, boarded the Mayflower in the fall of 1620. These people became known as Pilgrims. The Pilgrims sailed across the ocean and arrived in Plymouth, Massachusetts, in November. Many died on the voyage. More died during the first winter. Of 102 people who made the journey, fifty-eight died, including William's wife.

Within a year, William became governor of Plymouth Colony. He treated the non-Christian Pilgrims fairly, not giving anyone preferred treatment. He made friends with Native Americans who were native to the land. William explained the truth of the Bible to Squanto, who became a Christian. William later formed treaties with the Massasoit Indians and honored the agreements. William was so kind and fair that he was voted governor of Plymouth Colony on and off for thirty years.

You were called to be free, brothers and sisters; only don't use this freedom as an opportunity for the flesh, but serve one another through love.—Galatians 5:13

Defend Your Faith

William wanted a life where he could serve God and others without being thrown in jail. To enjoy this way of living, he traveled more than three thousand miles to find religious freedom. William didn't use this freedom to do whatever he wanted. Throughout his life, he looked for ways to build community and grow God's kingdom.

The religious freedom William helped establish is something we still enjoy today in the United States. Instead of taking your ability to worship freely for granted, take advantage of it. Invite friends to church. Look for ways to serve your neighbors. Try to live at peace with everyone. And remember to thank God for your freedom.

Defender Facts
Name: *William Bradford*
Place: *England and Plymouth Colony*
Time: *1590–1657*

HEART OF THE MATTER

Your brain controls what you say and how you move. Your brain even makes sure all your organs—like your heart, liver, and kidneys—function correctly. You don't even have to think about it! Aren't you glad you don't have to constantly remember, *Beat, heart, beat. Good job.*

Your brain is a big, beautiful thing. Scientists in Japan have discovered kids' brains are getting bigger. But before you start celebrating, it's not what you think. Doctors performed magnetic resonance imaging scans (MRIs) on the brains of nearly three hundred kids who liked watching TV. The scans showed that children who watched around four hours of TV per day had excess gray matter around their prefrontal cortex. Also called the *frontal lobe*, this part of your brain helps you make plans, solve problems, and develop your personality.

Scientists say building gray matter in this particular area of the brain is linked with lower verbal intelligence. Instead of big prefrontal cortexes, thin ones are better.

Studies show that most kids spend nearly five hours a day staring at a screen. Whether it's a TV screen, cellphone, computer, or tablet, you're feeding your brain all the time. Many of these activities don't fully engage the brain. Watching TV often results in zero brain activity. Researchers say playing an instrument, doing art, writing stories, and participating in other creative activities "exercise" your brain and help it thin the prefrontal cortex.

With everything your brain does, it's important to protect what goes into it. However, when King Solomon wrote about putting up defenses about what comes into your life, he said to guard your *heart*, not your brain. Why would he say that?

Above all else, guard your heart,
for everything you do flows from it.
—Proverbs 4:23

DEFEND YOUR FAITH

Back in Bible times, the heart was considered the location of knowledge. It's where your decisions were made and the source of the "true you." What a person's heart *desired* is what he did.

So when Solomon wrote to guard your heart above everything else, he was really saying, "Watch out for what you look at, think about, and allow into your life."

Guarding your heart doesn't happen by accident. In the New Testament, the Bible says to concentrate on whatever is true, honorable, pure, lovely, excellent, and praiseworthy (Philippians 4:8). Because the health and purity of our hearts are the most important things to God, ask yourself, *Are there any TV shows I should give up or songs and online videos I need to avoid?*

When we dig into God's Word, have a conversation with a friend, play a board game, or walk through nature, it builds our minds and protects our hearts in a good way.

WATCH OUT FOR JELLY

Have you ever dropped a glass jar of jelly on the kitchen floor?

Smash! What a mess. Jelly and glass everywhere. But what if you scooped a little of the "good jelly" from the mess and spread it on some bread? That'd make a good sandwich, right?

Wrong. When glass breaks, it creates broken pieces in every size and shape. Some might look like a half-broken jar. Others are the size of a potato chip. And some are like fine glass dust, sprinkled all over the place. Glass always breaks into different-sized pieces, but those pieces share one characteristic—they're sharp. Every piece, big or small, can cut you.

If a jelly jar breaks, ooey gooey jelly mixes with broken glass. There's no way to separate it out. Maybe the big pieces of glass can be removed, but there will always be smaller pieces hiding somewhere.

The Bible doesn't talk much about the science of broken glass, but it does warn of the dangers of tiny things that often go unnoticed.

Leaven makes dough rise. The most used leavening agent is *yeast*. These tiny single-celled organisms get mixed into bread dough to make it puff up. With warmth and time, the yeast grows and causes the dough to rise.

God created yeast and gave it the ability to make bread fluffy and delicious. These unseen organisms also keep you healthy by living in your stomach and helping you absorb vitamins and nutrients. Only a small amount of yeast is used in bread recipes—one hundred times more flour is needed. But this tiny ingredient truly affects, or infects, the whole loaf.

Don't you know that a little leaven leavens the whole batch of dough?—1 Corinthians 5:6

DEFEND YOUR FAITH

Sin is like the glass, or yeast, in our lives. It affects our whole being. Sin is a part of our fallen human nature and separates us from God. As followers of Jesus, we can try to pick out the big pieces of "glass." Maybe we stop lying to our parents or avoid thinking mean things about other people. These sins are obvious because they hurt us and the people around us. Other sins are tiny. We might not even know they're there, but their sharp edges still hurt us.

Because we can't rid ourselves from sin, it's great to know that Jesus sweeps away *all* the broken glass. When we admit that we're sinners who can't save ourselves and believe in Jesus, He comes into our lives and makes us clean.

James 2:10 says, "Whoever keeps the entire law, and yet stumbles at one point, is guilty of breaking it all." As Christians, it's good for us to follow God's laws and "clean up" the way we act. But we can't do it on our own. Fortunately, Jesus removes everything that sticks . . . like jelly.

WHAT DOES IT MEAN TO BE ADOPTED BY CHRIST?

The Humane Society estimates more than three million cats and dogs are adopted from animal shelters every year. Pets aren't the only ones waiting to be adopted. Over 125,000 children in the United States live in the foster care system, hoping for a forever home. Each year more than sixty thousand of these children will be adopted. Tens of thousands of other children get adopted in and from different countries around the world. Many of these kids go from a life of uncertainty into the care of permanent, loving families.

You may never know what it's like to live with a foster family or in an orphanage. But as believers in Jesus Christ, we know what it's like to be adopted into God's family.

Our adoption by the heavenly Father is one of the most incredible experiences of being a Christian. When we accept God's gift of forgiveness, we become His sons and daughters.

In the book of Romans, the apostle Paul says we receive God's Spirit when we're adopted as His children. Adoption is the legal process where a child is received into a family. The "adopter" assumes parental responsibility. The "adoptee" receives all the rights, privileges, advantages, and responsibilities of being part of that family.

When we're adopted by Christ, we become a joint heir with Jesus (Romans 8:17) and receive all the blessings, benefits, and privileges provided through His sacrifice. We can call out, "Abba, Father," just like Jesus did on the cross (Mark 14:36). *Abba* basically means "papa" or "daddy." By receiving God's Spirit of adoption, it allows us to call the most powerful being in the universe "Daddy."

DEFEND YOUR FAITH

Being part of a family also comes with responsibilities. You might do chores and help out your own family in different ways. As God's children, we need to be telling others about Him and sharing His love with a hurting world. God wants to see His family grow. He has plenty of room and love for everyone.

The best part about being adopted by Christ is the confidence it gives us of a future with Him. You have a forever home in heaven because you're a dearly loved child of God.

WORD PERFECT

Do you ever mack misstakes when you wright sumthing?

Everyone does. That's why pencils have erasers and computers have spellcheck. But none of those things were around when people were writing the Bible.

The sixty-six books that appear in the Bible were written over a span of 1,500 years. Kings, prophets, tax collectors, doctors, and fishermen all had a hand in writing God's Word. Biblical texts first appeared on scrolls made of papyrus or on animal skins. These were passed down among priests and memorized. Much of the Old Testament was written in Hebrew. A few sections of Daniel, Ezra, and Jeremiah were first put down in Aramaic. The New Testament was originally written in Greek.

With so many writers over so many years in so many languages and so many types of writing materials, it'd be easy to think God's Word would be riddled with mistakes. Yet scholars have concluded that the Bible we have today is almost 100 percent accurate to the authors' original writings. Pretty amazing, huh?

Scribes, the people who copied the Bible, often went letter-by-letter, word-by-word to create a perfect duplicate. No other ancient writing has the same amount of evidence to prove its authenticity.

How does it make you feel to know that historians and experts have concluded that the Scriptures are accurate? Does it give you more faith in its message?

The Bible was written and carefully protected, copied, saved, and translated by people who treasured it. God's Word has outlasted kingdoms, survived wars, and endured book burnings. And the most amazing part is that every word was inspired by the Creator of the universe.

All Scripture is inspired by God and is profitable for teaching, for rebuking, for correcting, for training in righteousness, so that the man of God may be complete, equipped for every good work.
—2 Timothy 3:16–17

DEFEND YOUR FAITH

Every time you open a Bible, you're opening a message from God written to you. Your heavenly Father loves you exactly as you are, but He also loves you too much to allow you to remain the same. Reading the Bible changes you . . . for the better. It helps you cut out behaviors that pull you away from God and replace them with wisdom and knowledge that draw you closer to Him.

How can you show God that you treasure His Word like the scribes and original writers? Maybe take a few minutes today to memorize one of your favorite verses. As you memorize the words, remember the power of God's Word. It's as alive, powerful, and true today as it was when it was written thousands of years ago.

A GOOD KING

The Bible tells us about a lot of bad kings. But Josiah was a good one. He started his reign when he was just eight years old and "did what was right in the LORD's sight" (2 Kings 22:2). In 2 Kings 23, Josiah reformed the nation of Judah. He tore down idols and burned them. He reminded the people of their covenant with God. He even reinstated the Passover, which hadn't been celebrated for four hundred years. During this massive cleansing of the nation and God's temple, Nathan-melech's name is briefly mentioned (2 Kings 23:11). It's the only time this temple official's name appears in the Bible.

In 2019, archaeologist Dr. Yuval Gadot unearthed a *bulla*, or ancient seal, at one of the largest ongoing excavations in Jerusalem, called the Givati parking lot site. He and his colleagues were able to translate the inscription, which read, "(belonging) to Nathan-melech, Servant of the King." Based on the style of writing and artifacts found around it, Dr. Gadot believes this seal dates to the sixth or seventh century BC. If this date is correct, this seal probably belonged to the biblical figure Nathan-melech.

Finding archaeological evidence that supports the Bible is always noteworthy. But this discovery is especially exciting because this bulla helps us remember a good king.

King Josiah called for God's people to remember. Reading the Scriptures and celebrating the Passover were meant to remind the people of the God they served and His faithfulness to them (Exodus 12:14; 2 Kings 22:8–13, 23:1–2).

About 650 years after Josiah re-established the Passover, Jesus celebrated the Passover with His disciples and gave us a new way of remembering. In Luke 22:14–20, we read about the first Communion. Jesus broke the bread and took the cup, declaring them to represent His body and

His blood. Then He commanded, "Do this in remembrance of me" (v. 19).

So then, brothers and sisters, stand firm
and hold to the traditions you were taught,
whether by what we said or what we wrote.
—2 Thessalonians 2:15

Defend Your Faith

Sometimes we can read Old Testament stories and think, *I'd never forget all those miracles and worship idols.* Jesus knew that even with the Holy Spirit living within us, we're still a sinful, forgetful people. That's why it's so important to pause to ponder Jesus' sacrifice during Communion, celebrate His birth at Christmas, rejoice in His resurrection at Easter, and contemplate His purposes for us daily as we read Scripture. Just like the people of Judah and their good king, Josiah, we need the rhythms and remembrances of traditions or we could easily forget important truths from the past.

Parents can pass down many things to their children. They may give their kids special recipes, family stories, furniture, money, and much more. One thing parents can't give their kids is their faith in Jesus.

Sure, parents teach about their faith. But it's up to each person to decide what to believe about Jesus. Our faith is a personal decision.

If you have parents or grandparents who followed Christ, that's great. But if you're the first person in your family to put your trust in Jesus as Savior, God loves you and can use you just as much.

The Bible tells many stories of first-time believers in families and people with a strong family heritage of faith. In the book of Acts, we meet a young man named Timothy who grew up in a faithful family. His grandmother Lois and mother, Eunice, had a sincere faith (2 Timothy 1:5).

Although his family believed in God, Timothy had to make the decision to follow Jesus for himself. Scholars believe Timothy met the apostle Paul in Lystra (Acts 14:8–23). Many experts believe Timothy was a teenager when Paul healed the lame man in Lystra and had to escape the city. Paul helped Timothy understand that Jesus was the promised Messiah, who came to forgive the sins of those who believed.

At the beginning of Paul's second missionary journey, he went back to Lystra and invited Timothy to travel with him to tell people the good news about Jesus. By this time, Timothy was most likely in his twenties.

Together, Paul and Timothy started churches in Philippi, Thessalonica, and Berea. But stepping out didn't come without persecution. Just like Paul, Timothy was beaten and abused for talking about Jesus.

After traveling with Paul for more than ten years, including another missionary journey, Paul left Timothy in Ephesus to take care of the church. At that time, Timothy was still considered young to be a church leader. But Paul knew Timothy had studied God's Word, knew the truth, and would be faithful.

Don't let anyone despise your youth, but set an example for the believers in speech, in conduct, in love, in faith, and in purity.
—1 Timothy 4:12

DEFEND YOUR FAITH

Paul's message to Timothy is the same one he would give to you: Just because you're young, it doesn't mean that you can't be an example to older people. Kids often have a huge impact on the lives of older family members and friends.

When you honor God with your speech, action, faith, and love, it sets you apart. People will notice and ask why you act differently than other kids. Then you can tell them about the transforming power of Jesus. Throughout Timothy's life, he lived up to Paul's encouragement to set an example. You can do the same, regardless of your age.

DEFENDER FACTS
NAME: *TIMOTHY*
PLACE: *LYSTRA*
TIME: *AROUND AD 30–90*

LOVE CONQUERS ALL

Love isn't just a good word; it's the best word! But the word *love* gets thrown around a lot. We love ice cream. We love our pets. We love our school. We love our parents. We love God. This single word—*love*—describes many feelings.

In biblical times, *love* was defined differently. Many words were used to describe different kinds of love.

The Old Testament has two Hebrew terms that have been translated into the word *love*.

- *Chesed* (hess-ed) is a covenant love. It's the type of faithful love that God has for His people.
- *Ahavah* (ah-ha-vah) is the type of love we have for ourselves or another person.

The New Testament was written in Greek, so the original writers used different words for love.

- *Phileo* (phil-A-oh) is the affection we feel toward a friend or family member.
- *Agape* (a-gop-eh) is the unconditional love God has for us. This is a committed love that lasts in good times and bad.

In 1 Corinthians 13, the apostle Paul wrote what has become known as the "love chapter." The word *love* appears ten times with Paul describing love as patient, kind, hopeful, forgiving, enduring, and never-ending. He also says what love is not: envious, boastful, arrogant, rude, self-seeking, and irritable. He ends by saying that love is the greatest.

Love is one of the most powerful forces on the planet. By understanding it, you'll be more prepared to express love in the way God intended. Your heavenly Father doesn't embrace cheap love. He wants you to love deeply and genuinely.

In the Bible, God is the object, motivation, and source of love. He is described as love (1 John 4:8). God shows His love for us in many ways. He expressed His love in the beauty of creation. He demonstrated His love by sending His Son to earth to pay the penalty for our sins. Jesus displayed ultimate love by dying on the cross and rising from the dead so we could be forgiven and personally know God.

Now these three remain: faith, hope,
and love—but the greatest of these is love.
—1 Corinthians 13:13

DEFEND YOUR FAITH

Go back and read the different definitions and characteristics of love. Do you always display these qualities? The Bible says people will recognize you as Jesus' disciple by the love you show (John 13:35).

Nobody is always loving. So don't worry if you mess up. But as you learn more about love, look for new ways to live it out.

Be quick to ask for forgiveness, show kindness, and be patient. Live selflessly and serve others. Those are things that God would love.

MIXED MESSAGES?

What would you do if you were unjustly put in prison?

Most people would wallow in misery, feel sorry for themselves, or cry. Not the apostle Paul. When he and Silas were thrown in prison, they prayed and sang hymns to God (Acts 16:25). God rewarded their faithfulness by sending an earthquake that loosened their chains and broke open the cell door.

The book of Acts describes how Paul constantly saw God protecting him during his four missionary journeys. In the face of angry mobs, hurling stones, shipwrecks, and snakebites, Paul seemed fearless. So when he felt "compelled by the Spirit" to go to Jerusalem in Acts 20:22, he was ready to go.

Paul jumped on a ship and sailed through several cities before arriving in Tyre. He stayed with some disciples in the city, and "through the Spirit they told Paul not to go to Jerusalem" (Acts 21:4).

Wait a minute! you may be thinking. *Is God's Spirit giving Paul two different messages?*

No way! God never contradicts Himself. God told Paul to go to Jerusalem and warned him that chains and afflictions would be waiting. Not a great selling point. In fact, most people would've turned and ran the other way. Paul chose to walk toward the uncertainty, saying, "I consider my life of no value . . . my purpose is to . . . testify to the gospel of God's grace" (Acts 20:24).

The disciples in Tyre received the same message from God: Paul would suffer if he went to Rome. Even though the Spirit's message was identical, they reacted differently. Instead of telling Paul to go into danger, the disciples warned him to stay away from suffering.

When you do what is good and suffer, if you endure it, this brings favor with God. For you were called to this, because Christ also suffered for you, leaving you an example, that you should follow in his steps.
—1 Peter 2:20–21

DEFEND YOUR FAITH

Sometimes being a Christian means taking the hard road. God probably won't call you to walk into your own imprisonment, like what happened with Paul. But at some point you may find yourself on a lonely path. Maybe you'll feel like an outcast for your beliefs. Your calling to follow Jesus may cause you to miss going to parties, not know the popular movies and songs, or feel left out in conversations.

Read today's verse again and notice three things. First, God wants you to do good. Second, your good actions may cause you some discomfort. Third, Jesus is your example for how to act.

When you make the right decision and suffer for it, it brings favor with God. Always strive to live in a way that honors Jesus by simply listening to His Spirit and following His example.

? IS GOD REALLY THERE WHEN BAD THINGS HAPPEN?

It's impossible to avoid pain in this life. The world isn't what it was supposed to be. God made it perfect. Man messed it up. But God didn't give up. He stayed committed to His creation.

But in the middle of tornados, wildfires, accidents, hardships, and pandemics, it can feel like God is far away. One family certainly felt that way when a wildfire burned down their home in Colorado Springs. Spurred on by sixty-five-mile-per-hour wind gusts and fueled by one of the driest winters in history, the fire also burned nearly 350 other homes in just a few hours.

Weeks later the family returned to their home, only to find a basement full of ash. They'd escaped with their lives but lost many of their possessions. Working with volunteers, they started searching for anything of worth. One evening as they were about to leave, the homeowner heard somebody shout, "I found something!"

A volunteer lifted an object from the rubble and handed it to the homeowner. Brushing away the soot, he saw the baby Jesus. In just a matter of minutes, the volunteer crew uncovered a porcelain nativity set of Mary and Joseph, some shepherds, a wise man, and even a few sheep.

For this homeowner, finding the baby Jesus in the middle of blackness and destruction was a reminder that Christ was still walking with his family. They'd lost everything, but they hadn't lost the most important thing.

Do not fear, for I am with you; do not be afraid, for I am your God. I will strengthen you; I will help you; I will hold on to you with my righteous right hand.—Isaiah 41:10

Defend Your Faith

When we look to God in our troubles, we find that He's always there to strengthen, help, and hold on to us. God is always with us, and He never leaves us.

Isaiah 61:3 tells us that God will give us a crown of beauty instead of ashes and splendid clothes instead of despair. You may encounter ashes and despair in this world, but know that God is with you. He'll lift you up, and He promises a future blessing.

Jesus came to earth to give you hope. God knew exactly what we needed when He sent His Son. Jesus is an amazing gift to the world. Our future is secure, and God's Spirit is always with us when we know Him. As you picture a tiny baby Jesus in the ashes, let it remind you that God is definitely there during your calamities. He gives you hope and can turn hard times into something beautiful.

It's About Time

How long is a year?

If you said "365 days," you're . . . wrong!

A year is based on the amount of time it takes Earth to make one full orbit around the sun. Scientists say a year lasts exactly 365.242199 days. That's 365 days, five hours, forty-eight minutes, and forty-six seconds.

Most years are 365 days on a calendar. But every four years we take a leap to make up for the lost time—a leap day that is. If we didn't add February 29 every four years, after one hundred years we'd be living around twenty-four days behind schedule.

People have been trying to figure out the correct time for thousands of years. About forty years before Jesus was born, Roman emperor Julius Caesar switched the old calendar to the Julian calendar. (Emperors loved to name stuff after themselves.) Forty-six days were added to the year 46 BC. However, communication was so slow that everybody wasn't on the same date until eight years *after* Jesus was born.

Then in 1582, Pope Gregory XIII ordered that everybody switch to the Gregorian calendar, which was more accurate than the Julian calendar. (That's what most of the world uses today.)

But even then, countries adopted the calendar at different times. When Sweden changed to the Gregorian calendar in 1712, the country had to add two leap days to catch up to the dates already followed by many nearby nations. That year Sweden celebrated February 29 *and* February 30.

Did you know time could be so confusing?

Don't overlook this one fact: With the Lord one day is like a thousand years, and a thousand years like one day. The Lord does not delay his promise, as some understand delay, but is patient with you, not wanting any to perish but all to come to repentance.—2 Peter 3:8–9

DEFEND YOUR FAITH

As Christians, we know God created time. Time is organized, steady, and unchanging—just like its Creator. However, the Creator of time isn't bound by time.

Sometimes when we pray it can feel like God takes forever to answer. God always comes through on His promises—whether it's His promise to answer prayers or to return to earth. Peter wrote today's verse in response to people who were frustrated by how long it was taking Jesus to come back. They wanted Him to return right away.

By waiting to return, God isn't showing that He doesn't care, but that He does. God is patient; He's waiting so more and more people can know Him personally.

God isn't on our timetable. He knows the best time for everything to happen. We can sometimes be impatient for God to answer our prayers, but all times are a good time to show patience.

DARE NOT TO COMPARE

Mirror, mirror on the wall. Who is the fairest of them all?"

You may recognize those words from the evil queen in *Snow White*. But kids everywhere look in the mirror and ask a similar question. Maybe you don't want to be the fairest, but you might compare yourself to your friends or the people you see in movies and think:

- *I wish my nose wasn't so long.*
- *I wish my forehead wasn't so wide.*
- *I wish I had more muscles.*
- *I wish my hair was wavy.*
- *I wish I looked like a model.*

Want to know a secret? Even models look in the mirror and see things they'd like to change.

Sounds silly, doesn't it? These people are paid millions of dollars for how they look, and they're not happy with their appearance.

The problem isn't with how we look, it's with who we compare ourselves to. The word **compare** means to look at two things to determine how they're the same or different.

Comparison may sound helpful. It is if you're comparing two choices of backpacks to buy for school. But comparing ourselves to others can be dangerous. Comparison often leaves us with an inflated view of ourselves or causes us to feel less valuable than others.

The apostle Paul warned of people who compared themselves to others and felt superior. That kind of comparison caused an inflated view of themselves.

We can fall into the same trap. *I give my old clothes to charity, and Liam doesn't even pray before meals,* we think. Instead of measuring our service to others, Paul said we need to evaluate how we've obeyed God's call on our lives.

When the standard is Jesus and God's commands in the Bible, we will always have more to strive for.

Let each person examine his own work,
and then he can take pride in himself alone,
and not compare himself with someone else.
—Galatians 6:4

Defend Your Faith

We don't only compare our actions; we also compare our appearances. Wishing we looked different doesn't help anyone, especially ourselves. When we look in the mirror, God wants us to see our reflection as one of His unique, wondrously made creations (Psalm 139:14).

God doesn't create cookie-cutter people. His creativity, beauty, design, and purpose shine through in every person. You are remarkable just the way you are. If you look at yourself as God sees you (and don't compare yourself to others), you'll gradually begin to understand that all of God's works are wonderful—including you.

ART OF A MIRACLE

During Jesus' ministry, the crowds that followed Him grew large. Really large. One day as Jesus preached on a mountainside near the Sea of Galilee, He noticed the crowd was especially huge . . . and hungry. Jesus asked His disciples, "Where will we buy bread so that these people can eat?" (John 6:5). Philip worriedly looked around. He knew the little money they had wouldn't buy enough to feed all the people.

Jesus wasn't worried. He knew the answer to His question. *Where would they buy food?* Nowhere. It'd be impossible to feed everyone.

But nothing is impossible for God. With a small boy's lunch, Jesus fed more than five thousand people and ended up with twelve baskets full of leftovers.

In 2019 a research team from the University of Haifa discovered a beautifully preserved mosaic that may be one of the oldest depictions of the miraculous feeding of the five thousand.

The mosaic was buried under a thick layer of ash at an archaeological site known as the "Burnt Church," about one mile from the Sea of Galilee. Experts estimate the church was built four hundred years after Jesus lived. The church burned down three hundred years later, collapsing the roof, which preserved the colorful mosaic. The artwork depicts two fish, five loaves of bread, and other items, including twelve baskets, pomegranates, apples, and flowers. Archaeologists believe this mosaic might indicate that early believers thought it was the site of the miracle.

Although experts may never be able to precisely determine the exact location, this mosaic proves that early Christians believed in and knew the details of one of the most famous events in the Bible.

DEFEND YOUR FAITH

Similar to the disciples, we often look at difficult situations with dismay rather than faith. When we pray, we may doubt that God can redeem a situation or help us in a time of need.

Even after Jesus miraculously multiplied this meal, His disciples continued to doubt. When they were trapped on a boat in the Sea of Galilee during a storm, they thought they might die (see Matthew 8:23–27). But Jesus came through again and calmed the storm.

We don't know what the people of the "Burnt Church" said when they saw their place of worship had been destroyed. They almost certainly didn't realize the ashes from the fire would preserve a piece of art as evidence of the truth in the Bible.

God has been redeeming hopeless situations for thousands of years. He'll do it in our lives too. We're always blessed and never hopeless.

LEAVING A GOOD SMELL

Have you ever stood near something that reeked? You probably got away as fast as possible.

People are attracted to good smells. Maybe that's why King Solomon wrote, "A good name is better than fine perfume" (Ecclesiastes 7:1). What you're known for matters. As a Christ follower, your reputation is important. For some kids, you may be the only Christian they know. Their opinion of you will influence their view of Jesus, so drawing people to you is much better than driving them away.

Although having a good name makes sense, the second half of that verse seems confusing: ". . . and the day of one's death is better than the day of one's birth." How could dying be better than being born?

To untwist this Scripture, looking at the surrounding verses helps. King Solomon was writing about the legacy that people leave when they die. Nobody can control the day they were born. But we do have the ability to influence what people will say about us when we're gone.

Thinking about the end of your life at your age may seem extreme, but that's the way God wants you to live. What do you want to be known for? It's not too early to start thinking about the legacy you want to leave for Christ.

*A good name is better than fine perfume,
and the day of one's death is better than
the day of one's birth.—Ecclesiastes 7:1*

Defend Your Faith

If you're having trouble coming up with what you want to be
known for, think about these qualities.

• *Conviction.* Know what God's Word says about right and
wrong, and live those beliefs. Jesus stood for His convictions to
the point of willingly dying on the cross.

• *Responsibility.* Do you make excuses or follow through
on your commitments? By admitting when you're wrong and
always being trustworthy, you'll stand out.

• *Understanding.* Jesus knew God. (After all, He is God.)
Understanding God and His grace is one of the most important
things we can do.

• *Encouragement.* How do you help your friends? Jesus
was the truest friend and made His friends better by
encouraging them to grow closer to God.

If you haven't already, make a plan to build and
then protect your reputation. When you take
the step to pep up your rep, you'll leave a
lasting legacy . . . and a good smell
on the people around you.

Zach had just moved to Tennessee, and everything seemed strange. There were new sights to see and new sounds to explore, especially the ones coming from next door.

Zach's neighbors tamed wild mustangs. One day he walked to his neighbor's house and offered to work for free if he could learn about horses. They agreed and allowed Zach to adopt a horse to train on his own. They even enrolled Zach into the local Youth and Yearling Mustang Challenge, where contestants between the ages of twelve and eighteen competed to tame a wild mustang in less than one hundred days.

Although Zach's horse lived on his neighbor's ranch, she was totally his responsibility. But days after starting training, Zach chose to go to a concert instead of care for his horse. When he returned home, the phone rang.

"Where are you?" his neighbor asked. "Why didn't you feed your horse?"

Zach rushed next door to apologize—and he learned something about integrity. His neighbor explained that integrity meant doing what you *should*, not what you want. It meant doing the right thing, even when nobody was watching.

Zach worked hard to prove he had integrity. He got up early for chores and training lessons. In the afternoons, he tossed hay bales. He worked until the heat made him dizzy. Every night he prayed with his dad for God's strength and endurance as he went to sleep with fresh bruises and aching muscles.

As Zach consistently showed up, his horse started to trust him. She began to listen to the sound of Zach's voice. He taught her lots of fun tricks, like how to take a bow, give Zach a hug, jump barrels, and walk a balance beam.

"Whoever is faithful in very little is also faithful in much, and whoever is unrighteous in very little is also unrighteous in much."—Luke 16:10

DEFEND YOUR FAITH

Zach learned the importance of being faithful in the little things. Every day his horse needed clean water and food. She needed to be combed, and the stable had to be cleaned. Plus, Zach had to work on basic training and building trust.

As Zach faithfully worked with his horse, his own faith grew. He realized as he consistently did the little things—read the Bible, prayed, went to church—that his own "wild" nature started to fade.

When we're faithful in the little things, we're able to hear God's voice more clearly. And by following His lead, we can do incredible things.

So how did Zach do in the competition? He and his horse swept all the events and won the grand championship. Showing integrity all summer had paid off. He was a winner . . . and you are too as you act with integrity and follow God.

DEFENDER FACTS
NAME: *ZACH*
PLACE: *TENNESSEE*
TIME: *MODERN-DAY*

*Q*uestions I have about God and the Bible . . .

Pursue righteousness, godliness, faith, love, endurance, and gentleness.—1 Timothy 6:11

Questions I have about God and the Bible . . .

Determine in your mind and heart to seek
the LORD your God.—1 Chronicles 22:19

Questions I have about God and the Bible . . .

Let the hearts of those who seek the LORD rejoice.
—1 Chronicles 16:10

Questions I have about God and the Bible . . .

A discerning mind seeks knowledge.
—Proverbs 15:14

Questions I have about God and the Bible . . .

_____

_____

_____

_____

_____

_____

_____

_____

_____

_____

_____

_____

_____

_____

_____

_____

_____

_____

_____

_____

_____

_____

Those who seek the LORD will not lack
any good thing.—Psalm 34:10

Questions I have about God and the Bible . . .

EQUIP THEM
— WITH —
TRUTH

Kids have a lot of questions about their faith.
So do their friends. The *CSB Defend Your Faith Bible*
equips kids to engage biblically and thoughtfully with
the most pressing questions they will face. Help your
young reader understand what they believe, why they
believe it, and how to defend it.

DEFEND
YOUR
FAITH
B I B L E

Digging into the Word: Travel to the Holy Lands and discover the historical evidence

Science in the Bible: See God's fingerprints all over creation

Untwisting Scripture: Discover the meaning and context behind difficult passages

That's a Fact: Go deeper with facts and stats that will help you understand more about the Bible

Defenders of the Faith: Read the fascinating true stories of people who have defended—or defamed—their faith

Know Question: Understand how to think biblically and critically about life's biggest questions.

FEATURES INCLUDE

Introduction to each book of the Bible

Presentation page for gift-giving

Part of the Apologetics Study Bible resource suite

Full-color interior featuring the complete text of the Christian Standard Bible®

The *CSB Defend Your Faith Bible* features the highly readable, highly reliable text of the Christian Standard Bible® (CSB). The CSB stays as literal as possible to the Bible's original meaning without sacrificing clarity, making it easier to engage with Scripture's life-transforming message and to share it with others.

Also available in Plum and Walnut LeatherTouch